Giallo!

THE SUNY SERIES

HORIZONS OF CINEMA

MURRAY POMERANCE | EDITOR

Giallo!

Genre, Modernity, and Detection in Italian Horror Cinemas

Alexia Kannas

Cover image courtesy of Photofest. Reprinted with permission.

Published by State University of New York Press, Albany

© 2020 State University of New York

All rights reserved

No part of this book may be used or reproduced in any manner whatsoever without written permission. No part of this book may be stored in a retrieval system or transmitted in any form or by any means including electronic, electrostatic, magnetic tape, mechanical, photocopying, recording, or otherwise without the prior permission in writing of the publisher.

For information, contact State University of New York Press, Albany, NY
www.sunypress.edu

Library of Congress Cataloging-in-Publication Data

Name: Kannas, Alexia, author.
Title: Giallo! : genre, modernity, and detection in Italian horror cinema / Alexia Kannas.
Description: Albany : State University of New York Press, [2020] | Series: SUNY series, horizons of cinema | Includes bibliographical references and index.
Identifiers: LCCN 2020018284 | ISBN 9781438480336 (hardcover) | ISBN 9781438480329 (pbk.) | ISBN 9781438480343 (ebook)

Subjects: LCSH: Detective and mystery films—Italy—History and criticism. | Horror films—Italy—History and criticism. | Motion pictures—Italy—History—20th century.
Classification: LCC PN1995.9.D4 K29 2020 | DDC 791.43/61640945—dc23
LC record available at https://lccn.loc.gov/2020018284

10 9 8 7 6 5 4 3 2 1

To Christos, who gave me my first Italian horror film, and the wrinkle in my brow.

Contents

List of Illustrations	ix
Acknowledgments	xi
Introduction	1
1 The Problem of Genre	9
2 The Cultification of the Italian *Giallo*	39
3 No Place like Home: The Late-Modern City	65
4 Those Who Wait: Tourists, Detectives, and Urban Experience in the *Giallo* City	89
5 The Most Unnatural Kind of Death	119
Conclusion	147
Works Cited	151
Filmography	159
Index	163

Illustrations

1.1 Fashion-house model Nicole (Ariana Gorini) poses with velvet-bound mannequins in Mario Bava's *Blood and Black Lace* (1964). Digital frame enlargement.   10

1.2 Industrial scientist Silvia Hacherman (Mimsy Farmer) attends a séance in Francesco Barilli's *The Perfume of the Lady in Black* (1974). Digital frame enlargement.   23

2.1 VHS cover sleeve of Fletcher Video's precertification release of Dario Argento's *Deep Red* (1975), rated X. Digital scan.   46

2.2 Uncut sexploitation, Charles Manson figurines and Italian horror on video: mail order advertisements on page 75 of *Psychotronic Video*, number 18, in 1994. Digital scan.   50

2.3 Lost masterpiece recovered: cover art for a 2012 release of Dario Argento's *Four Flies on Grey Velvet* (1971) from Shameless Screen Entertainment.   56

2.4 Death Waltz Recording Company's 2017 vinyl release of composer Bruno Nicolai's lush score for *The Case of the Scorpion's Tail* (Sergio Martino, 1971). Digital scan.   61

3.1 Journalist Andrea (Franco Nero) descends one of many spiral staircases in Luigi Bazzoni's *The Fifth Cord* (1971). Digital frame enlargement.   68

3.2 Tilde (Mirella D'Angelo) catches a glimpse of her murderer in *Tenebrae* (Dario Argento, 1982). Digital frame enlargement. 81

4.1 Roman local Marcello (John Saxon) shows American tourist Nora (Letícia Román) the beauty of the eternal city in Mario Bava's *The Girl Who Knew Too Much* (1963). Digital frame enlargement. 90

4.2 Nora (Letícia Román) tries to reconcile Rome's contradictory identities in *The Girl Who Knew Too Much* (Mario Bava, 1963). Digital frame enlargement. 94

4.3 Foreigner Sam Dalmas (Tony Musante) is caught off guard while strolling in Rome in *The Bird with the Crystal Plumage* (Dario Argento, 1970). Digital frame enlargement. 103

4.4 The tourist becomes the eyewitness in *The Girl Who Knew Too Much* (Mario Bava, 1963). Digital frame enlargement. 106

5.1 Eyewitness by design: Opera singer Betty (Christina Marsillach) is bound, gagged, and forced to watch the brutal set-piece murders in Dario Argento's *Opera* (1987). Digital frame enlargement. 120

5.2 Reporter Gregory Moore (Jean Sorel) plays detective in Aldo Lado's *Short Night of Glass Dolls* (1971). Digital frame enlargement. 132

5.3 Who was where, when? Marie's (Edwidge Fenech) friends discover her corpse in Mario Bava's *Five Dolls for an August Moon* (1970). Digital frame enlargement. 141

Acknowledgments

For the encouragement, support, and the inspiration they have offered, I would like to thank Melody Ellis, Ramon Lopez Castallano, Amy Clarke, Martin Evans, Adele Daniele, Bruce Milne, Craig Frost, Meg Johnston, Alexandra Heller-Nicholas, Stuart Richards, and Donna McRae.

This book began life as a PhD research project undertaken at Monash University in Melbourne, Australia, where I was fortunate to receive a teaching and research scholarship in the School of English, Communications, and Performance Studies. The project took longer than it should have, but it would never have been completed without the guidance of my supervisors Constantine Verevis, Adrian Martin, and Deane Williams; each made vital contributions to this work and I thank them for their ongoing support. Thanks also to Therese Davis, who provided invaluable advice during various stages of my candidature. To Susanna Scarparo and John Gregory: it was in your unit 'Italy on Film' that the seed for this project was sown—thank you.

During my candidature, I was fortunate to connect with a group of scholars on the other side of the world who I quickly recognized as "my people." Cult film scholar-stars Ernest Mathijs, Russ Hunter, Kate Egan, Peter Hutchings, and Jamie Sexton enriched my thinking and approach to this material via their own excellent work, as well as the detailed, provocative, and encouraging feedback they provided. Thanks also to the ever-inspiring Maša Peče.

The project took its current shape while I taught courses in cinema studies and critical writing in the School of Media and Communications at RMIT University. My thanks go to Lisa French, Patrick Kelly, Stayci Taylor, Adrian Danks, Stephen Gaunson, Peter Kemp, Smiljana Glisovic, and Djoymi Baker for their support and their friendship. Thank you also to my wonderful students who continually remind me how important it is to watch, to listen, and to write. I also gratefully acknowledge the stellar work of the staff at the AFI Research Collection: Olympia Szilagyi, Alex Gionfreddo, and Cathie Gillam, thank you for your wonderful support and enthusiasm.

In producing this book, I have had the great privilege of working with a scholar whose writing has long been a source of inspiration: thanks to my brilliant editor Murray Pomerance, whose intellectual generosity and patience know no bounds. Thanks also to Rafael Chaiken, Eileen Nizer, Michael Campochiaro, Gordon Marce, and the rest of the team at State University of New York Press.

And to Loris, James, Madeleine, Quincy, and Ryan: thank you for all your patience and love.

An earlier version of chapter 1, "The Problem of Genre," appeared in volume 5, number 2 of the *Journal of Italian Cinema and Media Studies* under the title "All the Colours of the Dark: Film Genre and the Italian *Giallo*."

Introduction

FRENCH WRITER/DIRECTOR DUO Hélène Cattet and Bruno Forzani's 2009 debut feature, *Amer*, imagines three key moments in its protagonist's life. The first part of the film introduces us to a child named Ana (Cassandra Foret) as she wanders the dark halls of her family's hilltop mansion on the Côte d'Azur. In one room, she encounters the corpse of an elderly man, from which she takes a gold pocket watch; afterwards, she imagines him awakening and regarding her with a horrific stare. Peering into another room further down the hall, she glimpses her parents having passionate sex. The film then leaps forward in time and we find that Ana (Charlotte Eugene-Guibbaud) is now a teenager, shopping with her mother in their village. The psychosexual tone established through Ana's witnessing of the primal scene in the first section of the film takes on a heightened potency now; as she saunters through the streets, her dress moving in the breeze, her nubile sexuality is put on display for the men of the village and Ana plays with this new dynamic system of looks she finds herself at the center of. In the third section of the film, the threat of *Amer*'s dark undercurrent materializes as a masked killer when Ana (Marie Bos) returns to her childhood home. The distinct three-part structure aside, *Amer* (which is French for "bitter") plays like a voyeuristic fever-dream, with almost no dialogue, sweeping lapses in time and close-ups that fetishistically fragment space and the body.

Most English-language reviews of *Amer* mention that Cattet and Forzani envisioned their film as an homage to the Italian popular film genre known as *giallo*. Stephen Holden's unfavorable review in the *New York Times*, for instance, calls the film "a surreal cinematic tone poem that pays slavering homage to Italian giallo horror films of the 1970s" (10).

Nigel Andrews at the *Financial Times* elaborates on the *giallo* influence, writing that *Amer* "is intended as a homage to the Italian, mostly city-set giallo films of the 1960s and 1970s—tales of murder and detection influenced by opera and grand guignol" (11). Jamie Dunn at *The Skinny* also foregrounds the stylization of the film in his review, calling it "a banquet of baroque imagery and kaleidoscopic colour." In his more nuanced reading of the film's multivalent relationship to its Italian genre lineage, Anton Bitel, in *Sight and Sound*, explains that

> *Amer* is a surrealist homage to the thematic preoccupations, visual stylings and musical cues of Italian genre cinema. Here all the primal scenes, sinister bewitchings, gloved killers and colour codings are borrowed from *gialli*, while the eclectic score has been appropriated directly from various 1970s *poliziotteschi*, and the beautifully styled erotica of the middle section recalls the fetishistic softcore of Tinto Brass. (46)

Although each of these reviews cites the fundamental importance of the *giallo* tradition to *Amer*, the writers' descriptions of this body of films are significantly diverse. The amorphous, polychromatic image that emerges from these divergent definitions is the subject of this book.

Giallo means "yellow" in Italian. To appreciate how a word that describes the color of sunflowers came to refer to a genre of violent, highly stylized crime films, we must begin in 1929, when Italian publishing house Mondadori released the first of a series of pulp crime and mystery novels they called *Il Giallo Mondadori*. Like the cheap "yellow-backs" published in Britain in the second half of the nineteenth century, the covers of the books in Mondadori's mass-marketed series were predominantly yellow. They proved to be so popular that in Italian the word *giallo* came to describe the crime and mystery genre as a whole. The first instalments of *Il Giallo Mondadori* were mostly translations of pulp crime novels by writers like Agatha Christie and Edgar Wallace. Film scholar Gary Needham tells us that the types of stories published as part of this original series were typically derived from two subgenres of mystery fiction: British Sherlock Holmes–style "rational-deduction" stories and "quasi-fantastic murder mysteries" ("Defining" 135), modelled on the work of Edgar Allan Poe. The great success of these cheap and highly portable volumes of pulp fiction soon instigated a wave of similar series being released in Italy by Mondadori's competitors and many of these sought to capitalize on the recognizability of Mondadori's yellow cover design. It was not long before the commercial viability of this new genre began to attract Italian writers who, for generic consistency, were often published using English-language noms de plume.

Italy's political landscape in the interwar period provided another reason for the surge in homegrown literary *gialli*: in its bid to protect the nation from the corrupting influence of the United States, the fascist government led by Benito Mussolini had, as Needham notes, banned outright the importation and translation of American hard-boiled crime novels, "on the grounds that their corrupting influence and glamorisation of crime would negatively influence 'weak-minded' Italians" ("Defining" 135). The dictatorship's stance on the importation of American culture meant that many Italian arts industries received substantial funding and flourished under its rule; it was in this period that Mussolini built Cinecitta—the largest and, at the time of opening in 1937, most technologically advanced film studios in Europe. Such initiatives helped the government to maintain rigid standards for content and censorship, but they also sought to actively encourage and nurture nationalist pride through the production of Italian versions of cultural products that would otherwise have been imported. The dichotomy created by this scenario came to be replicated, years later, in attitudes to the genre films that spring from these cheap paperback novels: on the one hand, imported and translated crime stories were dangerous, in that they opened the door to dissent and political transgression. At the same time, however, the Italian-authored *gialli* relied fundamentally on an association with British and American stories, as demonstrated by Italian authors' use of the nom de plume. From its very inception as a critical category, the *giallo* has occupied a curious state of in-betweenness.

As Mikel Koven has pointed out, in Italian "the term *giallo* acts as a metonym for the entire mystery genre" (2), so when, in 1962, director Mario Bava's Hitchcockian black and white murder mystery *The Girl Who Knew Too Much* was released, it was described as a *giallo*. This instantly apparent link to the literary genre also meant that Bava's film came to be known to many as the first "true" *giallo* film—or the place in which particular narrative and formal structures first coalesce to produce the cinematic genre. This basic narrative structure involves a protagonist who, after becoming an eyewitness to a violent murder, takes on the role of amateur detective. The murder witnessed is invariably one of a series of killings by a perpetrator whose identity the amateur detective works to uncover. Much of what comes to be known as the *giallo* genre's iconography is not developed until two years later, through Bava's 1964 *giallo*, *Blood and Black Lace*. It is in this second film that the level of violence escalates and we are introduced to what will become an archetypal characterization of the *giallo* killer: a mysterious, faceless figure who wears a black coat, a wide-brimmed hat, and, most famously, a pair of black leather gloves.

If Bava is responsible for establishing the codes of the cinematic *giallo*, director Dario Argento is most often credited with their refinement and popularization. His 1970 directorial debut, *The Bird with the Crystal Plumage* took Bava's blend of detection and stylized violence, twisted it in the direction of its contemporary art cinema, and became an international success. This confirmation of the financial viability of the genre set off a wave of *giallo* film production in Italy, with dozens of films being made relatively quickly and with fairly limited budgets. These were the conditions of production from which the corpus of the cinematic *giallo* genre emerged.

The approach I bring to this body of understudied films mirrors the unfolding significance they've had in my life, and, just like the narrative of *Amer*, this story pivots on three significant moments, or contexts. In the first, I'm a young teenager, asleep in my bed in Melbourne, Australia, late on a Friday night, when my father wakes me by whispering, "It's already started!" We sit on the couch wrapped in blankets in the dark, transfixed by the television screen, where the wind blows through the cemetery of the bucolic Italian town Buffalora, in the opening scene of *Dellamorte Dellamore* (Michele Soavi, 1994). This wasn't the first Italian horror film I'd ever seen, but it was probably the second. So, it was the moment when Italian horror, as a distinct category, crystallized in my mind, as well as the moment I decided I wanted to see as many Italian horror movies as I could. This obsession was nurtured by the late-night television programming of the Australian Special Broadcasting Service (SBS), whose emphasis on cultural diversity more broadly defined not only my introduction to Italian horror, but to Italian cinema itself.

Next, I'm nineteen, sitting on the floor in the summertime, flipping through a housemate's collection of stolen rental videos. They're mostly American slasher-cycle films made in the 1980s—video nasties like *The Burning* (Tony Maylam, 1981). But there is also a copy of *Deep Red* (1975), by Italian director Dario Argento. This part of the story I've told already elsewhere (see Kannas), but Argento's film played a significant role in my decision to take Italian Cinema as part of my arts degree at Monash University. For one glorious semester I spend my days watching Roberto Rossellini's *Rome, Open City* (1945) and Federico's Fellini's *La Dolce Vita* (1960), and my nights watching Argento's *Suspiria* (1977) and

Lucio Fulci's *The Beyond* (1981). I love it all, but this double life begins to generate some complex questions about the relationship between national cinemas and genre film.

In the final sequence, I'm twenty-three. Having just submitted my honors thesis exploring the notion of "operatic violence" as it relates to Argento's work, I sit down to review the year I have just spent focusing on the stylization of violence and trying to articulate what marked Italian horror as distinct from the other (mostly American) horror movies I had seen. I had watched wonderful movies about witches, zombies, and vampires, but what had become most interesting was the formal experimentation and reflexive tendencies that recurred through a particular subset of films revolving around crime and detection. I read photocopied cult film fanzines, trawled through online forums, and ordered bad quality DVD dupes and old VHS tapes via the internet—all of which pointed towards the existence of an Italian horror-crime-detection hybrid that could also be understood as a distinct genre. Where had it been hiding all of this time?

Because I had understood Italian horror first as Italian cinema, rather than "horror," the *giallo*'s near or total absence from key critical texts on Italian national cinema had surprised me as a university student. I soon came to realize that the "Italianness" of these films was marked by a sense of cultural illegitimacy. Unlike the canonized art cinema of directors like Fellini and Antonioni, *giallo* genre films were not seen as texts that make valuable contribution to discourses of Italian national cinema or identity. But the case of the *giallo* prompts us to question how the legitimacy of canonized Italian cinema has also determined the genre film's cultural value. Despite discourses of nation having had the power to marginalize the *giallo* genre from canonized histories of Italian cinema, a recent and traceable surge in critical and popular interest in *giallo* films—particularly in English-speaking contexts—demonstrates how a genre's status is never fixed. Retrospective festivals and *giallo* film seasons have propelled these once marginalized films into the critical spotlight. As a case study, the *giallo* thus also demonstrates how shifting audience and reception contexts have the power to reshape the reputation, status, and cultural value of popular cinema.

If my childhood fascination with Italian horror has helped to structure the questions I've asked of these films, so too has it affected my methodology. My encounters with these films did not occur in their country of production or in their native language; I discovered *giallo* films on the other side of the world, via sometimes censored versions on late-night Australian television, illegally recorded videotapes and cheaply purchased duped discs, up to forty years after the films were made. My reading of the Italian *giallo* has been structured by English-language cult film canons and discourses, and this has fundamentally affected the definition(s) of *giallo* I work with, as well as the selection of films discussed. If the descriptor "*giallo*" in Italian is a broadly applied generic term for crime fiction and detection narratives, used to refer both to films and literature, the use of this Italian word in English-language cult cinema discourse connotes a much more specific, if permeable, corpus of film texts. This critical category is delineated not only through the presence of crime or detection narratives, but also via a particular periodization. The high-volume Italian genre film production context that delivered Mario Bava's early *gialli* in the 1960s facilitated what is sometimes read as genre cross contamination, so that the *giallo* film as it is understood in English-language discourses contains not only elements of crime or detection, but of the horror film, too. This periodization, along with the influence of this critical category's most revered directors, Bava, Argento, and, increasingly, Lucio Fulci, also contributes significantly to the aesthetic and film style that comes to be associated with the Italian *giallo* film as it is understood by cult cinema discourses. The films I use for close textual analysis all speak to this particular definition of the *giallo* genre, as opposed to the broader Italian definition.

The shape of this book is asymmetric. The first part emphasizes the complex and ever-shifting nature of genre as it applies to the *giallo*, and the second explores some of the patterns of meaning that the generic structure opens up. The movement of this body of films through the critical shifts in each chapter is designed to recall the archetypical *giallo* formal motif: the zoom. Traversing space and time, this diachronic approach reviews the contestation around definition of this slippery group of films, but aims to move closer and closer to what constitutes its particular internal logic.

Chapter 1 uses the *giallo* as a case study to investigate the characteristics of genre as a system, by working through a number of models that scholars and theorists have applied to film genres in order to understand how they work. Building on theoretical frameworks developed by Rick Altman and Steve Neale, I aim to show that the *giallo* is uniquely positioned to highlight the limitations of evolutionary models of genre and, in fact, calls for a new conceptualization of the system that can account for the complexity of genre behavior. I argue that this is possible, and I draw on the mechanics of the kaleidoscope to help us understand how the system of genre produces ever-shifting, potentially infinite constellations of meaning, while simultaneously generating and maintaining patterns of recognizable family resemblances.

Chapter 2 maps a reception history of the *giallo* to consider how subsequent audiences and reception contexts have participated in what Rick Altman calls "regenrification" (*Film/Genre*). Evoking the dawn of the age of home video, this chapter is interested in how English-language audiences of the *giallo* helped to build and maintain the genre canon both as a concept and as an archive. Here I draw on newspaper reviews, fanzines, promotional material, cover artwork, and online forum discussion of *giallo* films in order to demonstrate how the process of regenrification renders *giallo* as a cult film genre. I also consider Jeffrey Sconce's work on paracinema in order to conceptualize the oppositional taste cultures in which Italian *giallo* films often find themselves participating. While such oppositional cultures have since been characterized as those that limit the texts they celebrate, here I position them as communities with fundamental agency in the process of generating and maintaining interest in such marginalized material.

Chapter 3 begins the second part of the book, which is interested in patterns of meaning generated through the genre system that relate to the critique of modernity. First I consider the cinematic city as it is imagined in the *giallo* films *The Case of the Bloody Iris* (Giuliano Carnimeo, 1972), *The Fifth Cord* (Luigi Bazzoni, 1971), *The Black Belly of the Tarantula* (Paolo Cavara, 1971), and *Tenebrae* (Argento, 1982), taking inspiration from Guiliana Bruno's idea of the city as a space that, much like genre, is constantly shape-shifting. I begin by considering how the *giallo* city is related to the city of *film noir*, using the concept of centrifugal space as defined by Edward Dimendberg to describe an increasingly decentralized city. I argue that *giallo* films, through their particular use of centrifugal space, both establish continuity between and distinguish themselves from earlier cinemas of crime and detection. Using Walter Benjamin's work on modernity and interiors, as well as Siegfried Kracauer's essay "The Hotel Lobby," this chapter reflects upon the architecture and living spaces of the *giallo* world, and suggests that their participation in the modernist aesthetic is characterized by their "lateness." The lack of warm domestic or personal spaces in *gialli* fuels a tone of ambivalence in these films, which I suggest reflects the tension at the heart of modernity itself.

Chapter 4 follows Nora, the protagonist of Bava's *The Girl Who Knew Too Much*, as well as Sam Dalmas, Argento's amateur detective in *The Bird with the Crystal Plumage* (1971), to consider how these characters function as avatars of urban experience in the late-modern *giallo* city. In both films, the role of amateur detective is fulfilled by an outsider, or tourist figure, who is ideally positioned to experience the city as a multifaceted construct. Drawing on Tom Gunning's work on cinema and modernity, this chapter argues that the *giallo* protagonist moves through three scopic regimes associated with modernity and urban experience: those of the *flâneur*, the *baudad*, and, finally, the detective.

Chapters 3 and 4 consider the *giallo* film's engagement with the conditions of modernity, but chapter 5 moves further in to explore the expression of this at the level of film style. It suggests that, despite the history of theoretical opposition between genre film and cinematic modernism, the *giallo* film's artistic critique of modernity is characteristically modernist. The complex history of defining cinematic modernism is explored through the prism of Susan Stanford Friedman's notion of "definitional excursions," where the project of fixing definitions is regarded with caution. This chapter foregrounds the formal strategies, such as reflexivity and abstraction, used in *gialli* to illustrate how these popular genre films use the same mechanics of cinematic modernism found in their contemporary art cinema. Here I seek to emphasize how cinematic modernism has so often been equated with the "masterpiece" that the genre film's valuable contribution to its discourses have been obscured. The final section of this chapter attempts to come to terms with the *giallo*'s particular engagement with cinematic modernism, and suggests that the *giallo* genre's baroque stylization and sense of decay articulate modernity's own *fin de siècle* moment.

Finally, a note on titles. Fans of the genre will be familiar with the typically evocative and often baroque film titles characteristic of *giallo* cinema; these are sometimes, but not always, translations from the Italian. *Giallo* films were also commonly given alternative titles for various international markets. For clarity, titles in this book reflect the film titles used most commonly in English-language cult cinema discourses, with Italian and alternative titles given in the filmography where relevant.

1

The Problem of Genre

IN 1817, SCOTTISH PHYSICIST SIR David Brewster patented an instrument invented to help educate observers in the basics of optics; he called it the *kaleidoscope*. The word is derived from the Greek καλός (beautiful), είδος (form), and σκόπιο (to see; tool for examination), to denote something like "an observer of beautiful forms." A handful of small transparent colored objects, such as glass beads, are transformed by light and the cylindrical toy's internal arrangement of mirrors to produce what Tom Gunning has called "a nearly infinite array of shifting symmetrical visual patterns, quite unrelated to . . . any claim of typicality" (Gunning 32). The saturated jewel-tones of patterns typically produced by the kaleidoscope recall the transparent, luminous palette of the stained glass window—and, for me, the opening credits of Italian director Mario Bava's 1964 film *Blood and Black Lace*.

This film's opening encapsulates so much of Italian *giallo* cinema's peculiar allure. The sequence's color palette transports the viewer at once to the dark world of the stylized *mise-en-scène* typical of the *giallo*; there are beguiling compositions that bathe the character's faces in eerie washes of deep rose or moss green as they pose, mannequin-like, with actual mannequins of deep red velvet who wear shiny black wigs. Bava uses the opening sequence vignette as a formal device to playfully introduce the forthcoming mystery's characters, but also to foreground the film's aggressive stylization from the moment it begins. Frozen in deliberate configurations of body and body-double, the characters and mannequins are arranged among the skeletal effigies of dressmaker's models in green, red, and blue, or beneath the abstract glitter of an out-of-focus chandelier, lit in twinkling chartreuse.

Figure 1.1. Fashion-house model Nicole (Ariana Gorini) poses with velvet-bound mannequins in Mario Bava's *Blood and Black Lace* (1964). Digital frame enlargement.

Confronted with the opening scene of this film that is regularly cited as one of the earliest examples of cinematic *giallo*, one begins collecting clues to arrange a system of expectation and hypothesis. Standing in the dark with their strangely lit faces expressing malice, naivety, or guilt, the characters appear to inhabit a baroquely ornamented rendering of the gothic horror film. But the vignette construction cuts through this moodiness; these characters tangled in what could be a murder-mystery have all the fullness of a playing card from the whodunit board game *Cluedo*, and the deliberate staging of their wooden poses create a distinct impression of self-consciousness. At the same time, there is something that very nearly overwhelms both these generic impressions; it is as if the film's style is leaking out, staining the surface of the film, which is perpetually threatening to explode in jewel-toned patterns. Like the first time you peer through that little hole in the end of a kaleidoscope, experiencing the opening sequence of *Blood and Black Lace* is utterly intoxicating.

Although the viewer new to *giallo* films may not yet recognize it as such, the peculiar, intriguing tone of this opening sequence is the ambience of the *giallo* world beginning to materialize: a world of crime, mystery, detection—and of madness, paranoia, alienation, and operatic violence. And, in its opening sequence, *Blood and Black Lace* offers us a number of clues that lead to mysteries far greater than those that occupy this single film's narrative. What is this strange, dark world that feels familiar yet antipodal all at once? How do we hold the ever-shifting image of it in our hands long enough to be able to trace its topography? If, as Rick Altman leads us to believe, "the entire history of genre theory has trained us to expect critics to start with a predefined genre and corpus" (*Film/Genre* 24), a consideration of the *giallo* as genre will require us to think through a group of films that have consistently eluded that very history. The questions raised by this complex problem are those that preoccupy this chapter. In what way do films called *giallo* belong to a distinct group that generates meaning through this membership? How do we begin to come to terms with the complexity of this set of films that seems to endlessly resist the manageable definitions that genre criticism has sought to achieve, time and time again? Taking such difficulties into account, is the *giallo* to be considered a genre at all?

The *giallo* makes a fascinating case study for genre theory for a number of reasons. Firstly, like most non-Hollywood genres, its existence has been almost entirely overlooked in the history of genre criticism. As a number of critics, including Dimitris Eleftheriotis and Alan Williams, have noted, genre theorists have historically turned, and returned, to the genre film output of Hollywood—and especially the western—in their attempts to decode the ways in which film genre operates. In fact, so great is the wealth of literature on the American genre film that one could be deceived into believing that the concept of film genre is entirely a Hollywood phenomenon. As Williams points out as early as 1984, however, to progress the work of genre criticism and to assert its validity in contemporary film studies, we need to begin to consider manifestations of film genre outside of Hollywood: "Crucially, we need to get out of the United States. Contrary to the impression given by books like [Thomas] Schatz's, 'genre' is not exclusively or even primarily a Hollywood phenomenon" (124).

The surge of interest in the Italian *giallo* film over the past decade has helped to reconfigure its status not only as a genre but also in terms of its position within the broader area of scholarship in Italian cinema. The academy's pervasive historical bias towards the European art film and its precursors has meant that the significance of the postwar period almost always pivots on the moment of neorealism and the canonized art cinema—of directors like Federico Fellini, Michelangelo Antonioni, and Luchino Visconti—that followed it, despite the nation's vast output of popular genre films during the same period. If the Italian *giallo* film has become more visible in the academy, it has been via its powerful association with the area of cult cinema rather than its absorption into the canon of Italian cinema. What is it about these (often) well-attended commercial releases that has precluded their significance to the construction of national identities? And what is happening, politically, when we disregard those popular cultural products consumed by a large percentage of the population?

Because the problem of *giallo* and Italian national cinema opens out onto these broader concerns, the genre is ideally positioned to help us push further into the terrain of genre theory. The task of arguing for the value of genre cinema—in discourses of national cinema or otherwise—necessitates an investigation into the mechanics of the system of genre itself. This means that our first concern is to come to terms with the system of "film genre"—as opposed to the "genre film." This qualification, as Schatz states, is necessary because the terms refer to distinct, but interrelated, entities; he writes that,

> whereas the genre exists as a sort of tacit "contract" between filmmakers and audience, the genre film is an actual event that honors such a contract. To discuss the western genre is to address neither a single western film nor even all westerns, but rather that system of conventions which identifies western films as such. (16)

Conceptualizing the *giallo* as such a system, we are able to think through its positioning in relation to a number of seemingly divergent discourses in order to show how these films harbor the power to pose fundamental questions about genre as a theoretical system, as well as to question the task of genre criticism as it has played out through history. As a case study of the ways in which genre behaves, the *giallo* shrugs off theories of generic evolution and nearly explodes the myth of hybridity; in fact, it asks for a conceptualization of genre that more readily accommodates the system's propensity to shift and change through time as films interact with film genre to produce meaning and cultural value.

The *giallo* is used here as a case study to explore the difficulties genre theorists and critics have faced in their attempts to come to terms with the complex patterns that systems of film genre produce over time. As this group of films comes into contact with each model, what I hope will become clear is the validity of the call made by Williams for a "radical" genre criticism that takes into account the difficult, often unpredictable and perpetually shifting nature of film genre. Building on theoretical frameworks developed by writers like Altman and Steve Neale, this book argues for that radical model—one that, in a number of ways, behaves like the mechanics of the same philosophical toy that Bava's opening credits recall: the kaleidoscope.

Writers have often returned to the idea of the kaleidoscope as a metaphor for the conditions of modern life; as Noel Gray points out, "The idea of bizarre images in jumbled disarray as a sign for the fragmentation of modern life and/or the loss of reality is a familiar metaphoric conception to us all" (11). Despite this, the kaleidoscope's use as metaphor has rarely been investigated as one that may provide a deeper understanding of other cultural patterns. In the case of *giallo*, the kaleidoscope metaphor works on two levels: it gestures towards the destabilized and fragmentary conditions of modern life that preoccupy these films, while, simultaneously, it describes the perpetually shifting nature of film genres like the *giallo*. I focus here primarily on the latter level. The quintessential modern optical toy reflects the ways genres work, because, like genres, the patterns it produces are fluid and unpredictable, yet always related to one another. It is useful as a metaphor for genre precisely because we can think about both genre and the kaleidoscope as "problematic[s] . . . made possible because the production of meanings generated by an image will always exceed the tight restraint of the designer's intentionality whilst appearing to remain forever tied to the graphic form of that intent" (Gray 96–97). What it offers for the study of film genre is not a new system for developing precise definitions, but a device that foregrounds genre's instability and fluidity. This shift from a commitment to rigid classification of film genres to a fragmented yet inclusive approach is a response both to Hollywood's hegemonic position in relation to the history of film genre studies, and to Williams's call for a "more radical" genre criticism (124).

Giallo, National Cinema, and Questions of Genre

> Those who inhabit nations with a strong sense of self-identity are encouraged to imagine themselves as members of a coherent, organic community, rooted in the geographical space, with well-established indigenous traditions.
>
> —Higson, "Limiting Imagination"

At one point, critical work on the *giallo* lived almost solely in publications and institutions dedicated to the celebration of cult cinema, B movies, trash, exploitation film, and horror movies. These spaces have been instrumental to growing and maintaining the visibility of *giallo* films, but have been less concerned with the tangled issues of genre and nation that the *giallo*'s identity brings up. Determining the *giallo*'s degree of "Italianess" in the face of such complexity is not the aim of this study, but some discussion of these problems is necessary in order to be able to move on to open up the films to new possibilities of meaning. While the *giallo* has been both celebrated and preserved in the canons of cult cinema, as Susan Hayward warns, "one must be aware of invoking an 'alternative' form of essentialism as a solution since, in the final analysis, it merely mirrors the practice of dominant ideology" (95). In other words, to consider the *giallo* genre only in relation to its cultness limits its potential to generate meaning.

To begin to open up some of the complex problems the Italian *giallo* film presents us, we might start by investigating the genre's characterization in scholarly maps of Italian national cinema. Peter Bondanella's seminal English-language history of the field, *Italian Cinema: From Neorealism to the Present*, first released in 1983, makes note of the careers of Bava and Argento in relation to what he calls the "spaghetti nightmare" film, which is framed "as a minor but intriguing variant of the mainstream Hollywood [horror] genre" that foregrounds "gore at the expense of coherent plots, complex character development, or subtle themes" (*Italian Cinema* 424). In this context the films are characterized by a focus on "special effects rather than mood" and a tendency to favor "grizzly scenes staged upon beautifully constructed sets that are edited and shot in an aesthetically interesting manner" (424). While Bondanella notes the spaghetti nightmare's formal experimentation and impressive stylization, the lack of attention paid to narrative is still framed as a deficiency, rather than a deliberate strategy. But where the incoherent plots of these films result in a lack of credibility, Antonioni's "slim" plots are perfectly acceptable—even when they take "second place to technique" (214). In celebration of the ambiguity of Fellini's oeuvre, Bondanella writes that "cinema entails expression, not the communication of information, and therefore its essence is imagery and light" (231), yet Bava and Argento's radical experiments in light are linked to B movie production values (424). Such readings of the landscape of Italian cinema—structured by the implicit binary of high and low art—are less representative of Bondanella than of the *giallo*'s status and perceived cultural value at a particular point in time. As the key text for English-language study of

Italian cinema around the globe, this book's survey of the field—which distinctly privileges certain kinds of films for inclusion in the national canon—was particularly influential. Through the first decade of the twenty-first century, this began to change: in 2009 Bondanella produced a new edition of this seminal text with the title *A History of the Italian Cinema*, which includes a chapter devoted solely to the Italian *giallo* film, along with a chapter on the Italian police procedural, both in addition to the original spaghetti nightmare material.

As the only popular Italian film genre that received sustained attention in English-language scholarship from the early 1980s, the spaghetti western has held a unique position in relation to Italian national cinema. This genre's inclusion in national cinema discourses relied on a major critical shift facilitated, to a great extent, by the pioneering work of British scholar Sir Christopher Frayling, who first wrote on Italian westerns and the genre's most celebrated auteur, Sergio Leone, in the 1970s and in 1981 released his pioneering book *Spaghetti Westerns: Cowboys and Europeans from Karl May to Sergio Leone*. Critical acceptance of these films as inherently Italian was also possible because films that traded under the Italian western genre label, especially those made by Sergio Leone, enjoyed both international popularity and favorable critical reviews in non-Italian publications. Being able to conceptualize the genre as a cycle in the historical trajectory of that most canonized Hollywood genre, the western, also rendered the films more easily digestible for non-Italian audiences who arrived at the cinema with a firm set of ideas about what a western might be. The ostensibly "pure" or classical form of the western developed in Hollywood made it easy to highlight the differences in the Italian westerns as the "spaghetti" or Italian inflection of the classical formula. But the *giallo*'s relationship with genres whose lineage it shares is more complex. Its textual qualities are drawn from the horror film, tales of detection, the travelogue, art cinema, stock footage, and the experimental film. If the spaghetti western stretches and twists the formula of the Hollywood western formula, the *giallo* breaks the genres it draws on into pieces and arranges these into new constellations for which traditional generic expectations are less helpful. Described variously as films of "blandly undistinguished material" (Combs), with "meager characterisation" (McGillivray) and "flat and predictable" scripts (Pirie) by the few English-language critics who did review *gialli* on their theatrical releases, these films have been historically framed as bad objects that sit outside the margins of the national cinema canon, despite the stylistic and formal crossover that happens across these lines.

While the period under discussion succeeds the moment of neorealism, it is impossible to create any kind of useful map of postwar Italian cinema without recognizing the impact this moment has had on the canon. Neorealist films were typically concerned with the difficult economic and moral conditions of post–World War II life in Italy as played out in the everyday lives of poor and working class citizens. The great impact of the neorealist film on histories of both Italian and international cinema more broadly has created a kind of model for culturally valuable cinema, prescribing particular thematic concerns and leaving behind stylistic legacies with which all subsequent cinema has had to contend. Despite these legacies, as most critical writing on the period suggests, there is no one set of defining characteristics or parameters that holds the neorealist films together as a "movement"; as Marcia Landy has pointed out, many of the characteristics associated with the neorealist moment can be identified in films of other periods, including earlier Fascist film productions. Reiterating some of the significant conventions associated with neorealist films here thus does not aim to fix a precise definition of this phenomenon, but to suggest its lasting impact on the constitution of the national cinema canon.

Films characterized as "neorealist" are typically cited as having been produced between 1945 and 1953, with *Ossessione* (1943), Visconti's adaptation of James M. Cain's 1934 crime novel *The Postman Always Rings Twice*, being the most important precursor to the moment proper. The films that coalesce under and around the term, from *Ossessione* to Vittorio De Sica's *Umberto D.* (1952), have enjoyed exhaustive critical attention, particularly in light of their appraisal in André Bazin's seminal essay "An Aesthetic of Reality: Neorealism," in which he anoints the Italian cinema as "the only one which preserves, in the midst of the period it depicts, a revolutionary humanism" (20–21). Describing the neorealist films as "reconstituted reportage" (20), Bazin imbues them and their historical moment with an immense significance for both the formation of postwar Italian national identity and the history of cinema itself, even when the majority of neorealist films did not perform well at the box office on release. This revolutionary quality—that promise of a new beginning—that Bazin sees, is echoed in the very title of Bondanella's earlier mapping of the nation's cinematic history, *Italian Cinema: From Neorealism to the Present*, in which neorealism is positioned as a point of origin, the mythical inauguration of a world-class national cinema.

The legacy of the neorealist moment can be summarized in terms of three broad shifts or developments in cinematic language that have been associated with the various films and directors considered under the blanket term. In the first instance, the formal innovations associated with these films have played a large part in the establishment of Italian cinema's world-class reputation as an innovative and poetic cinema. Neorealist productions typically eschewed the well-established filmmaking practices of studio-produced mainstream cinemas, such as continuity editing and the use of studio sets, in favor of a documentary aesthetic that aimed to reflect something "closer to reality." The films were characteristically shot on location in war-worn Italian cities or rural areas, where the difficult lives of everyday Italians could be illuminated and framed as allegories of the national struggle. Directors made use of multiple camera setups, disregarding traditional conventions of aesthetic continuity (such as maintaining the axis of action), which lent the politically loaded narratives a particular "liveness" and sense of urgency. These qualities were typically enhanced by the use of nonprofessional actors and, in particular, children, who came to symbolize Italy's future and the rebuilding of the nation. Such innovations helped to cement *neorealismo*'s status as a watershed moment in the history of world cinema, as well as establishing a yardstick for the social and political function of a "national cinema."

Although directors associated with neorealism worked in opposition to the mainstream cinema sanctioned by Mussolini's Fascist regime, paradoxically, their international success helped facilitate the surge in commercial cinema production in the years to follow. As both Robert Edmonstone and Christopher Wagstaff observe, new international audiences for the Italian cinema could be uncovered through the export and marketing of "prestige" productions like *Rome, Open City* (Roberto Rossellini, 1945), to engender a new image of the nation's cinema that was inexplicably linked to notions of quality. Many of the great directors associated with neorealism—including De Sica, Rossellini, Fellini, and Visconti—were, through the critical success of these films, elevated to the status of auteur. As authors of quality European cinema, they were ensured a long-standing international audience for their work, and enduring critical focus on their output in international film criticism. So central to the idea of Italian cinema did these names become that Millicent Marcus equates the death of Federico Fellini in 1993 with the death of Italian cinema itself (2002).

Finally, and perhaps most crucially, critical appraisals of the neorealist moment imbue this cinema not only with the power for social change and reform, but with responsibility for the depiction of the national story. In contrast to the "formulaic," "escapist" mainstream cinema produced contemporaneously, the neorealist film was a medium that gave voice to the despondent psyche of the war-ravaged nation—an "instrument," as Elio Petri claimed, "leading to knowledge about reality" (quoted in Mellen 10). For Marcus, who writes that "to preserve its integrity, film must engage in a continuous struggle to carve out and maintain an autonomous signifying field," the neorealist and postwar Italian cinema model moral engagement and epitomize the potentiality of the medium's specificity (8).

Stephen Crofts has argued that, while cultural specificity can never be defined exclusively by the boundaries of the nation-state, "at certain historical moments—often moments when nationalism connects closely with genuinely populist movements, often nation-building moments—national developments can occasion specifically national filmic manifestations which can claim a cultural authenticity or rootedness" (45). Crofts lists here the moment of neorealism as his primary example for this kind of manifestation, before drawing attention to a particularly significant repercussion of this kind of activity: that "such cinema 'movements' occupy a key position in conventional histories of world cinema, whose historiography is not only nationalist but also elitist in its search for the 'best' films, themselves often the product of such vital politico-cultural moments" (45). In other words, the canons of such conventional histories are constituted through highly selective taste formations that stress the subjectivity inherent in our understanding of notions of "quality." The product of what Crofts calls these nationalist and elitist historiographies is a canon of "culturally valuable" cinema that is filtered through these selective taste cultures. Such canons resist absorbing film texts that fail to conform to the expectations of those parent tastemakers, typically leaving in their wake those cultural products that threaten to contaminate the national cinema canon.

This points us towards the same question Andrew Higson asks in his study of British national cinema—namely, "Which strands or traditions of cinema circulating within a particular nation-state are recognized as legitimate aspects of the national cinema?" (*Waving the Flag* 63). It may be that if, as Higson expounds, "nationhood . . . answers to 'a felt need for a rooted, bounded, whole and authentic identity,'" what has been historically positioned as generic entertainment is felt to offer little response to this need for the national community (65). This need for a fixed or fathomable sense of what the nation might be is felt by what Benedict Anderson has termed the "imagined community": the community constituted by a sense of affinity members feel for one another. As Anderson puts it, a nation "is imagined because the members of even the smallest nation will never know most of their fellow-members, meet them, or even hear of them, yet in the minds of each lives the image of their communion" (6). The films canonized in traditional histories of the Italian cinema are typically those that function to stabilize and fortify this sense of communion between those who live in, or feel a relationship to, the nation-state. Neorealist films are seen as those that performed just this function at a critical juncture for the Italian nation-state as it began the mammoth task of repairing the physical and emotional damage caused by World War II. But as more recent scholarship in the area of national cinema has suggested, this conceptualization of the national community has some significant limitations. Higson explains that

> the "imagined community" argument . . . is not always sympathetic to what we might call the contingency or instability of the national. This is precisely because the nationalist project, in Anderson's terms, imagines the nation as limited, with finite and meaningful boundaries. The problem is that, when describing a national cinema, there is a tendency to focus only on those films that narrate the nation as just this finite, limited space, inhabited by a tightly coherent and unified community, closed off to other identities besides national identity. Or rather, the focus is on films that seem amenable to such interpretation. ("Limiting Imagination" 66)

The result of this tendency is the establishment of a canon, populated by particular, privileged films and directors whose legitimacy is reinforced through the repetition of this mapping. This process leaves in its wake a large body of films marginalized from the grand histories it creates. If, as Higson points out, the imagined national community is itself inherently unstable, we might reimagine a national cinema that better reflects the fragmented, ever-changing image of that community. Rather than privilege a cohesive body of legitimate texts that travel unchanged through historical epochs, we could think of the historically constituted canon and those texts it marginalizes in a dialectical relationship that does not seek to homogenize their differences but to interrogate their status and cultural value. If popular cinemas like the Italian *giallo* lack the moral accountability Marcus sees as integral to legitimate Italian cinema, this difference might present the perfect place to begin.

In considering the possible constitution of a British "national cinema," Higson outlines a number of definitions that aim to describe the various uses of the term (*Waving the Flag*). The fourth definition considers the idea in terms of representation. This approach to the discussion of national cinema is concerned with the narratives, themes, and motifs of the films in question and seeks to discern patterns of representation to ask questions such as "Do they share a common style or world view?" and "How do they project the national character?" Following this, Higson observes that the best way to explore such a perspective of national cinema might indeed be through the analysis of genre, where he argues that "the processes of repetition and reiteration which constitute a genre can be highly productive in sustaining a cultural identity" (5). Analysis of the patterns produced by genres can, in this view, offer significant insight into the culture that produces them. For Higson the genre film's formula acts as a kind of scaffolding—a productive framework for, rather than a disconnect from, the potential for critical questioning. While the exotic settings and jet-set lifestyle of the *giallo*'s characters may not mirror the life of the everyday citizen, this does not preclude the films from having something to say about the culture that produces them; "after all," as Higson points out, "questions of gender, sexuality and ethnicity, for instance, can be addressed in very poignant ways in displaced or exotic settings, whether the displacement is in terms of period or geography" (65). Significantly, such an approach also effectively bypasses the filter for "quality" texts that limits the scope of traditional histories of national cinemas, opening up possibilities for previously marginalized texts to contribute to such discourses.

There are two specific reasons why other Italian genres and genre films like the *giallo* may deserve the critical attention the Italian western has received. First, returning to Crofts's claim of the possibility of "specifically national filmic manifestations which can claim a cultural authenticity or rootedness" (45), we might begin to consider not only the watershed movement of neorealism, but also the phenomena of the spaghetti western, or the *giallo* also, as these kinds of national filmic manifestations. These genres are defined by their national specificity in their very naming: the prefix "spaghetti," like the word *giallo*, recalls not only the nation-state by which the films were produced, but also a unique rendering of what critics have seen as Italian incarnations of Hollywood staples. Despite its absence from so many historical accounts of Italian cinema's history, the *giallo* is regularly cited as a culturally specific hybrid of the investigative crime, thriller, and horror genres, with identifiable formal conventions that can be traced through a substantial body of films.

Second, the *giallo* genre's cultural value has been shaped—and reshaped—by the different reception contexts in which it has found itself.

Beyond its significance to Italian audiences during its peak period of production, the *giallo* has assumed a privileged position within English-language cult cinema reception contexts. This shape-shifting quality makes the *giallo* a fascinating case study for the ways that film genre itself is a system that produces ever-new patterns of repetition and difference.

Filone and Hybrid Forms

Recent scholarship on the *giallo* film—and Italian horror more broadly—has emphasized the use of the Italian term *filone*, instead of "genre," to describe this group of films. Meaning "vein," "streamlet," or "tradition," but also—as in Christopher Wagstaff's explication—"formula," the term *filone* helps to describe the particular production and reception contexts of Italian genre film in the postwar period. Mikel Koven's discussion of the *filone* also points to the connotations it carries in Italian phrases like "*'sullo stesso filone'* ('in the tradition of') or *'seguire il filone'* ('to follow in the tradition of')" (5). As David Church argues, both Italian and international commercially successful films functioned as "triggers" for *filone* cycles, where "some *filoni* capitalized on popular Anglo-American imports, some emerged after an Italian-made hit reinforced an Anglo-American one, and others were primarily imitative of homegrown Italian hits" (5). For the *giallo*, it was the success of Dario Argento's *The Bird with the Crystal Plumage* (1970), which crystallized the *filone* as a viable commercial formula.

Christopher Wagstaff's oft-cited work on the spaghetti western explains how the particular and complex "organization of production, distribution, exhibition and state support" in Italy between the mid-1960s and the mid-1970s facilitated a tidal wave of *filone* production (247), which scholars Stefano Baschiera and Francesco Di Chiara have thoroughly mapped. Nevertheless it is perhaps worth foregrounding here how the *giallo*'s exhibition contexts in particular differed from the ways genre films were disseminated in Hollywood. *Giallo* scholars have used Wagstaff's work to describe the three-tiered system of the exhibition classes in Italy, made up of the *prima* (first), *seconda* (second), and *terza visione* (third-run cinemas). Church explains that "whereas newly imported Hollywood productions would be released in *prima visione* . . . nearly three-quarters of the Italian film industry's total box-office receipts from the late 1950s to late 1970s were generated in . . . theatres located in small cities and towns of outlying provinces" in the *seconda* and *terza visione*

(5). The *gialli filone* would have screened across these various "levels," with films by well-known directors like Bava and Argento mingling with Hollywood releases and European art cinema in the *prima visione*, while a range of lower-budget *gialli* were made specifically for the second and third-run houses.

What conceptualizing the *giallo* as *filone* enables is the flexibility to consider a wide range of films prone to consistent deviation from any established generic norm as nevertheless being part of the same discursive group. Edmonstone suggests that popular genre films produced during this period in Italy cannot be neatly organized into genre-specific piles, because the conditions of production mean that particular characteristics—like the presence of "brutality"—flow laterally across film groups, from peplums to *gialli* to police procedurals. In this way, the concept of *filone* opens up flexibility for genre critics engaged in the project of categorization, because it considers the boundaries of definition not as fixed, but porous structures. Mark Betz goes further to suggest that, because of this lateral flow, the idea of the *filone* is "of potentially great value as a methodology for understanding, in stylistic as well as historical terms, the developments of art cinema in Europe in the postwar era and its confluence with what have previously been regarded as supplementary exploitation *codes* of *display*, of *content* and of *affect*" (513). In Betz's view, this flow is not confined to the realm of genre film production and textuality, but leaks across the precarious boundaries between high and low art.

Thinking *gialli* as *filone* also means that films are considered for both their difference from and their repetition of the dominant features of the *giallo* formula. This acknowledges the complex relationships at work in this body of films, without having to commit wholly to a rigid set of defining semantic elements and syntactic relationships to which the films often do not adhere. For instance, Bondanella's chapter on *gialli* defines them as "mystery, detective, or thriller films" and draws a definitive line that excludes *gialli* featuring supernatural agents of cause and effect (*History* 374). But the flexibility of the *giallo filone* has accommodated such films as *The Perfume of the Lady in Black* (Francesco Barilli, 1974), an occult/psychological thriller in the vein of Polanski's 1970s apartment-based films, which featured in the *giallo* program of the 2007 Melbourne Underground Film Festival and which sometimes turns up in fan-authored *giallo* film lists. With no real murder mystery plot, the threads that tie this film to the *filone* include the use of actress Mimsy Farmer who had starred in Dario Argento's influential *Four Flies on Grey Velvet* in 1971, as well as the authorial presence of director Francesco Barilli, who had worked as a writer on Aldo Lado's *giallo* of 1972 *Who Saw Her Die?*. Aesthetically, *The Perfume of the Lady in Black* follows in the tradition of Bava's saturated use of colored light and ornate mise-en-scène.

Likewise, fan-authored lists of *giallo* films also often include Paolo Cavara's *The Black Belly of the Tarantula* (*La tarantola dal ventre nero*; 1972), despite the presence of its police officer protagonist, Inspector Tellini (Giancarlo Giannini), rather than the "amateur detective" more commonly understood to be a marker of the *giallo* film. As Koven points out, films that adopt the investigative perspective of the police are usually categorized as police procedurals, or *poliziotto*—a separate *filone* of the Italian popular cinema (7). But *The Black Belly of the Tarantula* works in the tradition of the *giallo* by positioning Inspector Tellini as an outsider in the police force, while hitting other key *giallo* marks with its gloved and traumatized killer and Morricone score.

The *filone* makes fluid what we might usually think of as *hybridity*: a descriptor used in both academic and less formal discourse to describe films or film genres that appear to combine dominant elements from multiple recognizable "root genres" in a kind of genre cocktail. Frequently described as a hybrid of the horror, thriller, and detection genres in English-language criticism, the *giallo* film or *filone*'s production conditions suggest a fertile ground for all kinds of cross-pollination to take place.

Figure 1.2. Industrial scientist Silvia Hacherman (Mimsy Farmer) attends a séance in Francesco Barilli's *The Perfume of the Lady in Black* (1974). Digital frame enlargement.

But, as Eleftheriotis suggests, the notion of hybridity as it relates to film genre needs qualification and complication. While genres like the *giallo* do mix patterns from recognizable Hollywood genres, explaining this activity as hybridization can rely on the problematic supposition that these American root genres are essentially pure. This understanding of hybridity depends on what Janet Staiger in her work on post-Fordian Hollywood calls a "historicist fallacy" that is "compounded if the past pattern is assumed to be pure against a visible present that is not, that the visible present is some transformation, deterioration, or hybridization of a pure essence and origin" (6). This fallacy is enacted in the case of the *giallo* when it is understood as an Italian mix of Hollywood genres.

For Staiger, hybrids are possible when Hollywood genres, as dominant discourse, are mixed by "minority or subordinated groups that use genre mixing or genre parody to engage dialogue with or criticize the dominant. Films by US feminists, African-Americans, Hispanics, independents, the avant-garde, and so forth might be good cases of internal hybrids," and cross-cultural mating across national borders could also produce hybrid genre forms, she argues (17). While critical consideration of cross-cultural pattern mixing is valuable and necessary work, the language of generic hybridization can also work to reinforce dominant ideologies of authenticity and originality. And, in the case of European popular cinema, such rhetoric reaffirms Hollywood as the producer of original or pure forms. Referring to the spaghetti nightmare as a "minor . . . variant of the mainstream Hollywood genre," the use of the word "spaghetti" as a descriptive term marks out these films' Italianness through a farcical association between stereotypical Italian cuisine and a classic Hollywood genre, producing an Italian-flavoured hybrid genre (Bondanella *Italian Cinema* 424). In his work on the spaghetti western, Eleftheriotis highlights the repercussions of such cavalier classification when he writes, "'Spaghetti' here not only connotes inferiority and foreignness but also contamination as a dangerous and degenerate impurity. In this way, merely as a generic classification, the Italian engagement with an American genre is precluded to be an inferior, impure and contaminating exercise" (92). Film genre theory's historical reliance on the Hollywood genre film has limited opportunities to destabilize this hegemony.

When framed by this Hollywood-centric understanding of hybridity, the *giallo* reads as an incomplete cultural form, or as a trace of some lost or absent whole; in other words, the *giallo* becomes a fragment. Gray argues in his work on the kaleidoscope that the fragment refers always to "a piece of a whole or incompleteness," where the "fragment itself is either valued as less because it is not whole, and/or, is valued as 'more than' because it is all that is left of some 'original whole' and therefore must stand in for this whole" (100). The tendency to read the *giallo* as an "incomplete" or "broken" artefact is evident even in celebratory criticism, which frequently champions the genre's characteristic lack of interest in coherent or cohesive narrative. For James Gracey, this quality is evident in Argento's work when "logic is lost in a constant bombardment of extravagance and perversely alluring stylistics" (11). Similarly, Tim Brayton, author of the blog *Antagony and Ecstasy*, writes that "instead of a coherent mystery narrative *Black Belly of the Tarantula* has style by the bucketful" (2009). Juxtaposed with canonized Italian national cinema that affirms a "rooted, bounded, whole and authentic identity," these highly stylized and fragmented *giallo* films read as illegitimate cultural products (Higson 65).

The *giallo*'s brokenness has been thought both as willfully determined and as a product of ineptitude, and it is worth clarifying this distinction. Drawing on the work of Mikhail Bakhtin, Eleftheriotis argues for the notion of "intentional hybridity," which "involves the deliberate production of hybrids that challenge the unity and authority of monological forms" (98–99). Intentional hybridity foregrounds the fluidity and cross-pollination between groups of texts that the *filone* inherently allows for, treating these not as simplified organic or inevitable processes of "culture mixing," but as deliberate hybridizations occurring amongst the already "impure nature of culture" (99). This more nuanced reading of hybridity encourages us to see value, rather than an assemblage of broken parts or fragments. As with the kaleidoscope, the result of hybridization is always a new whole image:

> Whilst the composite image formed in the kaleidoscope is obviously made up of many images they are not incomplete pieces of some whole. Rather, they are multiplications of the initial scene open to the view of the kaleidoscope. What is produced by the multiplication is a visually whole-image, not an incomplete piece of some previously imaged-whole. (Gray 100–01)

Understanding the *giallo filone* as an intentional hybrid, rather than a "composite secondary form" (Eleftheriotis 100), will help us to frame the textual specificities of this group of films, to understand how they relate to their multiple contexts, and to uncover their significant cultural value.

Filone and Value

While the concept of the *filone* offers a useful critical framework to help us understand relationships between films, what the shift from genre to *filone* also achieves, however, is a reinscription of Hollywood's dominance in the mapped history of genre film production, and within the history of film genre criticism as it has largely been narrativized. Because the concept of *filone* foregrounds the *repetition* of particular motifs, themes, creative personnel, and aesthetic trends between the various films (across what we would consider separate genres), they are unable to be recognized as the kinds of "coherent, value-laden narrative systems" that traditionally constitute genres (Schatz 16). The shift from genre to *filone* also does little to alleviate tensions around the *giallo* film's position in relation to matters of taste and value. Wagstaff notes, for instance, how most Italian films considered to belong to *filone* have been "dismissed as *sottoprodotto* [by-product]," or "a debased, ersatz product" (248). Despite his insistence on finding a more accommodating term to account for the behaviour of this group of films, Koven also maintains that the *giallo* film—with its mystery plot stamped from a commercially successful formula, produced quickly and cheaply in response to audience desire and ticket sales—is inherently "disposable" (79). This understanding of the *giallo* as a product of formula finds its ultimate conviction in "The Do-It-Yourself Giallo Generator," a web page that randomly configures a *giallo*-esque title, director's name, and plot line each time the page is reloaded. The novelty of this application lies not only in the absurdity of the randomly generated phrases, but in the correlation between them and actual English-language titles of *giallo* films, which can easily match the bizarre quality of those titles randomly generated. Characteristically, the formulaic nature of the generator means that the novelty soon wears off; the title and accompanying paragraph of bizarre plot produced randomly for a moment of amusement, is entirely disposable. Like the pulp-novels from which it took its name, the *giallo* film is also often seen as a commercial product designed for single-use only.

As Raphaëlle Moine acknowledges in her 2008 book *Cinema Genre*, this attitude to the function of genre formula is one deeply entrenched in film criticism; for some critics, generic expectations elicit effects more ruinous than boredom. Moine quotes from a 1993 text by French film critic Barthélemy Amengual, who likens the exchange between genre film and its audience to a kind of extortion, whereupon the film demands from the viewer a "blank sheet of paper that they sign without determining the content" (88). Amengual's concern stems from the idea that generic systems dictate audiences' construction of meaning by generating reductive expectations. In broad theoretical terms, this assumes that the key to genre cinema's pleasure lies simply in its innate compulsion to repeat; it underestimates genre film audiences' generic literacy and discounts the pleasures of *difference* audiences may experience when encountering familiar genres. In the case of *giallo*, this association with formula speaks principally to the films' narratives, subordinating the other, more salient, aspects of film form. This reinstates an all-too-common hierarchy that, as fans have often pointed out, may miss the point in reading the *giallo*; as Bondanella writes, "If the *giallo* sometimes fails to live up to the high standards of art film narrative in its plotting and the characterization of its protagonists, it privileges, on the other hand, dramatic visuals and music" (*History* 375).

To understand the *giallo* as *filone* is to understand, synchronically, key differences between the systems of production generating genre films in Hollywood and Italy in the postwar period. But to explore the ways these films—as genre or *filone*—generate meaning necessitates a diachronic approach: one that considers how the phenomenon shifts and changes through time. With the perspective offered by the framework of the *filone*, we can undertake the critical shift back to a consideration of *giallo* as genre. In fact, thinking about the *giallo* in relation to established theories of film genre demonstrates how its apparently difficult behavior is replicated by all film genres.

Genre and the *Giallo*

In his review of Hélène Cattet and Bruno Forzani's 2013 neo-*giallo*, Jason Anderson suggests that the opening of *The Strange Color of Your Body's Tears* functions as "a primer on the semiotics of the *giallo* film," after which the directors "rapidly proceed down the lurid checklist of essential sights that no self-respecting exercise in the genre could do without." This checklist recalls those fan-authored lists that include motifs like black leather gloves, demented children's dolls, disembodied eyes, and the gleaming blade of a very sharp knife. Certainly, *The Strange Color of Your Body's Tears* has all of these, or what Anton Bitel refers to as "the grammar [and] iconography . . . of the sensationalist mystery genre known as *giallo*" (review of *Strange Colour*). It quotes "classic" Argento *gialli*, from *Deep Red* (in the husband smashing through his bathroom wall) to *Tenebrae* (in the pair of shiny red pumps in his missing wife's closet). For Michael Atkinson, what Cattet and Forzani offer here is "a unique recipe for meta-giallo," but this is a recipe for formal style more than a list of motifs, one which makes use of "paintbox flourishes and slivered reflections, Art Nouveau designs, and stop-motion still montages, edited together in a rambunctious associative flow that doesn't tell a story so much as arterially spray one across a sumptuously papered wall." As the reviews of *The Strange Colour of Your Body's Tears* illustrate, Cattet and Forzani's film draws on the aesthetically distinctive style of the *giallo*: a term that serves as an index for a group of films that are clearly understood by these critics—and the filmmakers themselves—to constitute a genre.

In his article "Playing with Genre: Defining the Italian *Giallo*," Gary Needham writes that "the term itself doesn't indicate, as genres often do, an essence, a description or a feeling" (135). Unlike the western, whose principle setting is revealed in its generic naming, the genre index *giallo* does little to describe the narrative formula, thematic concerns, or aesthetic style of the films it names. Mary Wood suggests that films that take up the word "*giallo*" as a descriptive indicator often display "the use of saturated yellow tones on film to connote hidden realities and to introduce the intertextual frames of generic conventions into the text" ("Italian Film Noir" 236); however, this treatment of color is not a typically cited feature of the genre, and is particularly absent from many of the better-known *gialli* by directors like Argento and Bava, who tend to favor palettes of higher contrast.

Although the Italian word *giallo* may not serve as a simple index of any textual characteristic or aesthetic quality for English language audiences, for fans the term points directly back into the genealogy of the genre, because it references the distinctive yellow covers of those pulp fiction paperbacks released by Mondadori that were the first *gialli*. This lineage provides an aesthetic trope that is picked up on by video and DVD companies, who have released a number of cinematic *giallo* titles with covers featuring what Wood describes as "garish illustrations on a yellow background" ("Italian Film Noir" 250). Anchor Bay's 2002 DVD release of *The Giallo Collection*, provides a key example: the artwork for *The Bloodstained Shadow* (Antonio Bido, 1978), *The Case of the Bloody Iris* (Guiliano Carnimeo, 1972), *The Short Night of Glass Dolls* (Aldo Lado, 1971), and *Who Saw Her Die?* (Aldo Lado, 1972) all feature hallucinogenic vignettes from each of the films encircled by a thick red line, stamped onto the front of a bright yellow cover. This marketing strategy, devised to exploit cult audience interest in and knowledge of the genre, demonstrates that for particular user groups, the naming of the genre refers to the mystery narratives found in those portable and "disposable" pulp fictions (Koven 79). The *giallo* film itself can also self-consciously work through this lineage, as in the opening of Bava's *The Girl Who Knew Too Much* (1963), where future amateur detective Nora Davis sits on her Rome-bound airplane reading a murder mystery novel. As Church points out, in addition to these Anglo-American literary roots, the *giallo filone* has "roots in a variety of transnationally circulating texts," including Hitchcockian thrillers and "West German *krimi* films of the 1960s—a cross-cultural translation of influences which," he argues, "helps to account for the conflation of horror and *giallo* films in Anglo-American criticism since the 1970s" (7).

While the myths and evolutionary lifespans of Hollywood genres like the western have been established through academic interrogation, the *giallo*'s iconography, or lists of dominant textual themes, motifs, locations, and character types, and the syntactic relationships these form, have been assembled primarily through fan discourses. The introduction to Nigel Burrell and Paul Brown's independently produced publication *Giallo Scrapbook* is typical of this kind of discursive activity genre fans regularly participate in: they ask, "What constitutes a giallo?" and proceed to lay out a set of flexible parameters that form a kind of list:

> To be classified into this genre the film needs to have a twisted character killing in the most bizarre and inventive ways, usually dressed in black with semi-obligatory black gloves. The murder weapon is usually a very sharp instrument of terror, a blade of some kind, probably a knife or straight-razor, but it can be anything, depending on how resourceful the assassin is at the time (a cat whose claws have been dipped in poison comes to mind!). The victims are usually attractive and are mostly of the female kind. The plot will involve some kind of trauma or elaborate idea that triggered the killing. And the deaths will be spectacularly gory and quite often of a sexual nature. And most importantly, the film is Italian of origin, although there have been several copycat variations from various other countries. . . . The *Giallo* also stands for style, this can be the glorious widescreen compositions, the dizzying and intrusive camera angles, the splashiest blood you ever saw,

the continual bevy of beautiful damsels in distress, and even the soundtracks which could warrant another volume just to discuss. (Burrell and Brown 2)

While a good number of the *giallo*'s identifying characteristics listed by Burrell could be argued to be dominant features of other broader genres (such as the horror film, or the thriller), it is their particular synthesis in the *giallo* film that convinces the critic of the stability, and thus existence, of this distinctly Italian genre.

The kind of fan-authored quasi-scholarly critical activity typified by Burrell's outline finds its theoretical match in the model of genre described by Altman in his 1984 article "A Semantic/Syntactic Approach to Film Genre." He explains here that while semantic genre definitions that depend on lists of common motifs, settings, and traits have the benefit of being inclusive in their formation of canons, their broad applicability limits their potential to generate meaning. Because the *giallo* shares so many identifying characteristics with Hollywood genres like the horror film or the thriller, a semantic approach offers "little explanatory power, [but] it is applicable to a larger number of films" (10). Thus, while such approaches actively participate in establishing and expanding the canon, rarely are they able to advance the project of understanding the more ephemeral meaning-making processes at work in the genre system. Even if we can agree that *giallo* films typically contain traumatized killers wearing black leather gloves (although some, like *The Perfume of the Lady in Black*, do not), what else can we use such membership to explain?

If semantics are the building blocks of genre, syntactic models are more interested in the way these blocks are arranged and the patterns that emerge from this activity. Altman points out that while this second approach may allow the critic to decipher a "genre's specific meaning-bearing structures" (10), it lacks the potential for broad application, and is thus unable to explain more lateral relations between genres and genre films. Syntactic approaches to genre are typified by work on the Hollywood western by writers like Jim Kitses and John Cawelti, who argue that the genre pivots on relations such as the dialectic between culture and nature, community and individual, future and past, and so on. Altman argues that the semantic and syntactic models might be more productively used to describe genres when they are combined. By drawing on their complimentary nature, he is able to come to terms with what he calls "the necessarily dual nature of any generic corpus" (11). This is the model used in Koven's study of the *giallo*, where he identifies semantic consistencies across a broad range of films called, or related to those called, *giallo*, before drawing conclusions about these patterns in relation to issues of dominance, frequency, and perceived use. These semantic building blocks include isolated or confined settings, such as *Blood and Black Lace*'s villa, or the apartment building of *The Case of the Bloody Iris* (Giuliano Carnimeo, 1971), and the omnipresence of icons of modern transportation like the airplane and automobile, discernable throughout the *filone*. Recurrent character types include the killer who is motivated by a past trauma and the amateur detective, who becomes embroiled in the plot as an eyewitness, and, often, through some key misrecognition or failure of vision. The primary syntax of the *giallo*, then, according to Koven, is that the genre displays "an ambivalence toward modernity" (46). We will return to this tension that the *giallo* harbors in relation to the conditions of modernity in chapter 3.

Genre and Change

Altman's dual approach also aims to counter the issues generated by film genre theorists' reliance on semiotic models that do not take into account the passing of time; as he explains, "Genre theory has up to now aimed almost exclusively at the elaboration of a synchronic model approximating the syntactic operation of a specific genre" ("Semantic/Syntactic" 12). Here history is viewed as "a discontinuous succession of discrete moments, each characterized by a different basic version of the genre," which is understood as "a different syntactic pattern which the genre adopts" (12). These patterns are understood using various devices, including the notion of "classic" or ideal representations of the genre, as well as through the authorial signatures of particular directors whose films are seen to embody such representations. Limited English-language critical attention has mostly left the *giallo* without a delineated "classic" period, but this tendency towards a truncated evolutionary historiography is revealed when Bava is referred to as the "father" of the *giallo* genre, or when Argento's films are seen as "exemplary" of the *giallo* genre. It is worth adding that because of the Italian exhibition structure, audiences would not necessarily have encountered the *giallo filone* in the linear manner this evolutionary trajectory describes, which again reminds us of the reconstituted nature of such histories.

The most commonly offered explanation for film genres' propensity to change through history is rooted in our most significant experience of time as human beings: that is, genres are often understood to have *lifespans*. This structuring of genre occurs in both academic and less formal responses to films and film genres; it surfaces whenever we argue about a genre's first textual entry (Which film is the first true *giallo*?), or are seduced by the proposition of uncovering its precise moment of death (What year was the last *giallo* film made?). But if, as Schatz suggests, genre is a system of conventions by which genre films are understood, and if such understandings are developed through a multiplicity of subjective readings, carving a clearly delineated lifespan into a genre's tombstone becomes a messy and potentially futile affair.

Another biology-derived approach used by genre critics has involved mapping generic developments according to patterns of evolution. When genre texts begin to display a new or changed emphasis on certain semantic/syntactic relations, this shift is understood as the marker of a new stage in the genre's lifespan. Sitting at the pinnacle of such models is Schatz's theory of generic evolution; published in 1981, it leaves in its wake a trail of residual assumptions about and attitudes to genre that require some unpacking. The aim here, as Moine puts it, is "to put an end to the theory of generic evolution," but in doing so, we need to understand how such models have played into the ongoing impulse to cement definitions in genre criticism (132).

Schatz describes the changes genres undergo as "patterns of increasing self-consciousness," where each shift is marked by a greater level of self-awareness; in order to be able to track this evolutionary lifespan for any given genre, he develops a map of ways this evolutionary patterning typically unfolds. Although the process involves what he calls "both internal (formal) and external (cultural, thematic) factors," through iterations of repetition and refinement, the genre story's "basis in experience gradually gives way to its own internal logic" (Schatz 36). Schatz's schema for the lifespan of film genres is built around four distinct phases, drawing on the work of art historian Henri Focillon:

> A form passes through an *experimental* stage, during which its conventions are isolated and established, a *classic* stage, in which the conventions reach their "equilibrium" and are mutually understood by artist and audience, an age of *refinement*, during which certain formal and stylistic details embellish the form, and finally a *baroque* (or "mannerist" or "self-reflexive") stage, when the form and its embellishments are accented to the point where they themselves become the "substance" or "content" of the work. (46)

Schatz's schema finds some resonance in *giallo* fan discourse. This conventional wisdom most often cites Bava's *The Girl Who Knew Too Much*, from 1963, as the "first *giallo*," thus aligning it with Schatz's experimental stage, where the genre conventions are being established. If Argento produces the exemplar of the *giallo* genre, we might equate the beginning of the "age of refinement" with his first *giallo* success, *The Bird with the Crystal Plumage*, in 1970.

But evolutionary models may be less useful in accounting for some kinds of generic development, as Rick Worland illustrates in his introduction to *The Horror Film*, where he attempts to map the generic evolution of the horror movie with this evolutionary schema. Here, a key problem for the horror film's lifespan surfaces in 1959 with vampire-western *Curse of the Undead* (Edward Dein). Positing the film as a simultaneous moment of refinement for both the horror and western genres, Worland asks, "Is *Curse of the Undead* so outlandish and exceptional that it spilled over from mere refinement into what Schatz terms a genre's baroque stage?" (19). Steve Neale ("Westerns and Gangster Films") has pointed to the fact that even some of the earliest westerns display degrees of self-consciousness, upsetting the evolutionary process the western genre is supposed to have undergone. Most significantly, the way canons are developed via taste formations they also work to perpetuate also means that films with the potential to challenge evolutionary models might be disregarded. For instance, Sam Newfield's musical western *The Terror of Tiny Town* reflexively exposes the semantic/syntactic elements of the western genre by casting "Jed Buell's Midgets," a performing troupe made up entirely of little people. Released in 1938, during the western's so-called "classic stage," this single film problematizes the western's evolutionary schema—but only if it is taken into account. As an exploitation film and box-office flop, since featured in books such as Harry and Michael Hedved's book *The Golden Turkey Awards*, published in 1980, *The Terror of Tiny Town*'s power to challenge such models has lain dormant because it is an *illegitimate* western.

Worland describes the Baroque stage of genre development as the moment when classic genre "elements have become so familiar they can no longer be considered natural but rather inevitably noticed as artificial and played out" (20), but the opening credits of *Blood and Black Lace* signal from the film's outset a highly developed reflexive and self-referential character; qualities that the rest of film eagerly maintains. *Blood and Black Lace* understands already the contract of expectations between itself and its audience, and is able to honor this while engaging in reflexive formal experimentation. Perhaps more than many other genres, *giallo* films harbor this sense of "playing out" their own conventions from the moment the genre emerges as a recognized system. From its inception, cinematic *giallo* engages reflexively with its roots in literary tales of mystery and crime, and with earlier and contemporaneous Italian and global cinema positioned across the spectrum of taste. Through the framework of the *filone*, these lateral connections are multiplied. This generates a group of texts that have, in some sense, always already undergone the processes of evolution when they emerge as a recognized system.

Another strategy to clarify genre's propensity to change through time is to conduct a synchronic analysis. Rather than provide an evolutionary map of the genre, Koven's study of the *giallo* builds a snapshot of the conditions of production and exhibition of *giallo* films in Italy in the 1960s and 1970s. In this context, he examines their common traits and themes. But the problem of history resurfaces when this reading of the *giallo* as "vernacular cinema" invokes what Susan Hayward has called an "alternative form of essentialism" (95). Koven argues that because *giallo* films were not designed to be consumed in the contemplative manner associated with art cinema, they cannot be productively analyzed using the same methods. While canonized Italian art cinema warrants critical reconsideration year after year in academic books, journals, study-guides, and retrospectives, the vernacular cinema model fixes the *giallo* to a specific (imagined) historical moment and preserves the genre's lack of integrity. No matter how the artefact is fixed, however, there is always more than one way to read it. If film genre is a contract between the film and the audience, it is a contract being perpetually revised. Sitting in the cinema to watch Argento's *Deep Red* in 1975 in Italy, in 1984 in the United States on video, or in 2013 at the Melbourne Cinémathèque, we all sit down to watch (a version of) the film Argento made, but the text potentially offers each of us different pleasures that relate to this multiplicity of contexts.

The issues generated via the meeting of transhistorical film genres and their audiences are revisited by Altman himself, when, in his book-length study *Film/Genre*, he concedes that "assuming stable recognition of semantic and syntactic factors uncross an unstable population, I underemphasized the fact that genres look different to different audiences" (207). This highlights two significant issues. First, no matter how Italian audiences understood *giallo* films—and the genre more broadly—at the time of their original theatrical release, this "original" audience is only ever a scaled-down imagined community, riddled with the very same problems Higson elucidates in his exploration of the instability of the "national" ("Limiting Imagination"). Second, as Altman points out, genres are used in diverse ways across diverse audience groups, differentiated across both space and time. While the genre critic can learn from analysis of diverse audiences and their uses of genre, she cannot fasten down the kaleidoscope of meaning-making processes to prevent new constellations of meaning. If the *giallo* film today finds itself wandering the halls of the Anglo-academy, it has been shepherded from Italian cinemas of the 1960s and 1970s by a multiplicity of users, including cult film audiences, who participate by constructing and reading these perpetually shifting meaning-making structures and patterns.

Because the *giallo* genre is "equally at ease with opera and comics, the art of statuary and fashion design, aestheticism and sleaze, realistic violence and abstract stylization," as Philippe Met points out, this group of films functions as "a perfect illustration of the degree of arbitrariness, ambiguity, instability or, worse, fallacy, inherent in any given generic categorization, theoretical systematization, or notional definition" (197). Even if we see the potentiality of textual hybridity, how do we begin to recuperate the value of genre theory and criticism once the system of genre has been rendered infinite in its potential to generate meaning? Staiger qualifies her rejection of the purity hypothesis by making clear that to expose the ahistorical fallacy of generic purity is not to deny the existence of patterns within genres. In fact, she argues that "patterns provide valuable material for deviation, dialogue, and critique," going on to explain that,

> although the tactics of grouping films by genre have been eclectic, grouping films can still be an important scholarly act because it may elucidate what producers and consumers of films do. That is, they see the films against a hypothesized pattern based on viewing other films. The *process* of comparison—which requires pattern—is crucial to communication and may contribute to enjoyment of a text. (6)

Instead of narrativizing the lives of genres in order to explain perceived trends, it might be more productive, taking our cues from Staiger, to think of generic change as an ongoing process of pattern production. It is here, in regards to this idea of process, that the metaphor of the kaleidoscope provides a most useful model.

Drawing on Paul Ricoeur's definition of metaphor as a concept with two registers—the "like" and the "not like," Gray shows how the kaleidoscope is "like" the "ever-changing nature of change" because "it fulfills the requirements of 'is like' by supplying to the viewer a constantly ever-changing pattern like that witnessed in ordinary perception" (100). Where the optical instrument fulfils the "not like" requirement of Ricoeur's idea of metaphor in relation to change more broadly is that the presentation of these perpetually shifting patterns occurs within the confinement of the apparatus itself. To consider the kaleidoscope as a metaphor for genre is different, because the system of genre itself functions precisely as that apparatus of confinement; that is, like the kaleidoscope, film genres produce "an ever-changing image. . . . Yet this imaged process is forever confined" (Gray 100). To follow through with Ricoeur's definition of metaphor, we might say that the kaleidoscope is "not like" the system of genre in that the apparatus physically limits the number of fragments from which the perpetually shifting composite images are produced, whereas systems of genre—especially in the case of the *filone*—are theoretically unrestrained by space or time, and thus open to absorbing a potentially infinite number of new qualities in the creation of their composite "images." Like the apparatus of the kaleidoscope, the system of genre produces ever-new whole texts that bear varying degrees of likeness and unlikeness to the images or texts that produced them. This process of change that produces patterns of meaning plays out in infinite configurations, but is held together by the apparatus of the genre system, which is sometimes invisible, and has a multiplicity of locations. The role of the genre critic, then, is to uncover and analyze instances of patterning and, as Staiger concludes, their "social, cultural, and political implications" (17).

"To Live Historically": Genre Critics and the Problem of Definition

Eleftheriotis points out that, despite the abundance of work in areas of genre theory and genre criticism, the role the genre critic plays is a problematic rarely attended to (93). But reflection and self-awareness on behalf of the genre critic could be key to progressing the work of genre theory and maintaining the validity and currency of genre criticism, for, in the final analysis, it is the problem of definition that halts these projects. Film genre theory has always had to contend with limitations inherent in the activities of categorization and definition, whether the object of analysis is the Hollywood western or the Italian *giallo* film. Because the *giallo* seems to resist easy categorization, it has found itself on the margins of both canonized Italian cinema and genre cinema. Yet, as both a group of films and a system of conventions for understanding those films, it displays patterns—particularly in relation to the conditions of modernity—that can be analyzed and compared to produce highly valuable cultural critique. As critics who perform such analysis, we momentarily freeze history in order to be able to say something meaningful about the genre or the genre film, but without accepting that such suspensions can only ever be temporary, we enact Staiger's historicist fallacy. Without such perspective, genre criticism locks the genre to a moment of history that has always already passed.

Robin Wood has written about the difficulty and importance of critical approaches that do not commit exclusively to any one way of approaching the text, instead remaining open to drawing on a multiplicity of theoretical positions. For Wood, the difficulty of such an approach pivots on its lack of a rehearsed critical framework, which problematizes "the validity of evaluative criteria that are not supported by a particular system." Wood asks:

> For what, then, *do* they receive support? No critic, obviously, can be free from the struggles and tensions of living to some position of "aesthetic" contemplation. Every critic who is worth reading has been, on the contrary, very much caught up in the effort to define values beyond purely aesthetic ones (if indeed such things exist). Yet to "live historically" need not entail commitment to a system or a cause; rather, it can involve being alive to the opposing pulls, the tensions, of one's world. (59)

Being alive to the kaleidoscope of ambiguities, contradictions, and tensions inherent in these films so concerned with the conditions of modernity, seems key to understanding the *giallo*'s patterns as constellations of culturally valuable signs. And being alive to history seems the necessary condition of a radical genre criticism.

2

The Cultification of the Italian *Giallo*

Walking across the ground level of Melbourne Central shopping center in late 2018, I looked up to see an advertisement for Luca Guadagnino's 2019 remake of *Suspiria* beaming from an enormous digital billboard suspended from the glass ceiling in the center of the mall. The striking, limb-spangled promotional still from one of the film's avant-garde dance set-pieces hovered uncannily between the center's multilevel concourses—visible from every balcony, as well as from the ground. The text on the screen declared that the "reimagined masterpiece is a seductive monster," describing Guadagnino's film as the director's "take on Dario Argento's classic . . . [with] horrors and charms all its own." The promotional copy is careful to differentiate Guadagnino's version from the 1977 film in an attempt to legitimize the recent remake in the eyes of horror fans, while it also positions Argento as the esteemed director of the original film, now a "classic masterpiece." As Russ Hunter has shown, *Suspiria* is the film that most often represents the "critical highpoint" of Argento's career, but this promotional evocation of the Argento brand suggested an elevation in the director's cultural value more broadly (65). I wondered if Argento now feels the same way as renowned *giallo* director Sergio Martino, who, in a 2017 interview, said that "when Tarantino playfully knelt in front of me, and in front of all my colleagues, at the Venice Film Festival . . . I thought: is he kidding me? But in reality it was a belated recognition. It was like sitting on the riverbanks and seeing the body of the enemy float by" (Olesen 265).

The belated recognition of Italian directors who worked within the *giallo filone* stems from a traceable shift in the status and visibility of the films that has been particularly noticeable in English-language reception contexts. Raiford Guins has argued that this is the result of "remediation," or the ways that new technologies have motivated new understandings of Italian horror as a category. Guins sees the availability of Italian horror (including *giallo* films such as *Deep Red*) on video, and then on DVD, in terms of two distinct periods that produce different understandings and definitions of the category for North American audiences. For Guins, the trajectory of this shift traces the Italian horror film's transformation from (VHS) "gore-object" to (DVD) "art-object," effectively enacting what Rick Altman refers to as "regenrefication" (*Film/Genre* 203). But the concept of "remediation" can also oversimplify the story of the *giallo* film's shifting cultural value.

First, is worth extending Guin's reception chronology in both directions; since the publication of his essay on the remediation of Italian horror, Mikel Koven has suggested that the key to understanding these films lies in the specificity of their original exhibition contexts and intended theatrical audiences. But 2006 also saw the release of the first Blu-ray disc titles, and soon this new technology was ushering in another wave of *giallo* film releases and re-releases, only to be followed a decade later by the introduction of ultra-high-definition Blu-ray and 4K resolution, which effectively redoubled opportunities for packaging *giallo* films and Italian horror as collectible "art-objects." Each of these moments can be productively considered in terms of their participation in the *giallo*'s ongoing "remaking." Second, we should consider the wider range of factors that have contributed to the changing status of these films; as Jamie Sexton has pointed out, while technologies have been important to the *giallo*'s regenrefication, we shouldn't underestimate the level of agency cult film fans and media collectors have had in directing discourses of value (21).

Italian Audiences

Since the 1992 publication of Christopher Wagstaff's influential work on the industrial conditions and audiences of the Italian western, there has been a tendency for English-language scholarship to narrate the exhibition history of the Italian *giallo* as a story that begins in the *terza visione*, or third-run, cinemas of Italy's small rural towns. Koven, for instance, describes his book *La Dolce Morte* as a synchronic investigation of the *giallo* film as "vernacular cinema," where both the genre's production of meaning and its cultural value are shaped by the exhibition trends Wagstaff describes. In Koven's view, the audience who frequented the *terza visione* theaters in the 1960s and 1970s represents the *giallo*'s target demographic, and he suggests that the films were consciously designed for this particular mode of consumption. But, as Thomas Schatz reminds us, genre films and film genres are not necessarily located in the same place, and fixing the *giallo* film to a particular time, place, and audience has significant impact on the films' meaning-making processes.

As one of the many *filoni* being produced in the Italian film industry throughout the 1960s and into the 1970s, the *giallo* is often described in terms of its contribution to the wave of cheaply made genre movies that flooded the market during this period. Fueled by the box office success of key films like *The Bird with the Crystal Plumage*, dozens of *gialli* were made in this period to capitalize on the sudden popularity of the formula. As Wagstaff explains, the majority of these quickly and cheaply made films were exploitation movies destined for the local cinemas of Italy's small towns and provinces, rather than the first-run cinemas located in major cities. David Church points out that the lion's share of these were shown in the "*terza-visione* theatres located in rural and southern areas, where daily programming changes were common due to the shortage of television sets in working-class households" (5).

For Wagstaff, third-run cinemas in regional areas represent a particular reception context, where the audience is defined by both their lower-class socioeconomic status, as well as their particularly casual mode of engagement with the films being screened. In contrast to the hushed stillness we might usually associate with theatrical screenings, the *terza-visione* audience was more likely to drink, smoke, and chat while the film was being screened. This audience's engagement is typified by the notion of the "distracted gaze"—a mode of spectatorship characterized by continual glancing away from, and then returning to, the screen. The *giallo* film exemplifies what Koven calls "vernacular cinema," because the films' violent set-pieces are specifically designed to draw the distracted (lower-class) gaze back to the screen, while narrative-driven sections allow time for lower levels of audience engagement. For Koven, analysis of the Italian *giallo* film must take into consideration this intended reception context, and investigating the genre according to alternative sets of values misses the point, because "vernacular cinema is an exceptionally obvious cinema" (39). In the case of the *giallo*, this fixes a particular mode of spectatorship to a particular class of viewer, a scenario that, for Koven, shapes both the intention of the filmmakers and the most suitable approach to take in the critical analysis of the film texts. Such histories of cinematic spectatorship rely on Anderson's "imagined community," in that they assume an audience homogeneity that can only ever be imagined, and this image of the "vernacular" audience certainly wasn't the way all *giallo* directors imagined their audiences. In a 2015 interview, director Sergio Martino answered Giulio Olesen's question about his audiences by explaining:

> I never rely on a specific target; I imagined an audience that was going to the cinema not to get bored. This did not mean that they were not culturally evolved. When I walked into theatres, I often saw upper-class people that were there to enjoy themselves, perhaps with their wife looking for strong sensations. In fact, my films were also shown in the first run cinemas and I often went there to see the reactions in the audiences. If audiences did not choose American films, it was thanks also to Dario Argento, who was the first to succeed in Italy with *gialli*. Actually, when I did my first *giallo*, *Next!* (1971), Argento had recently released his first movie, and my film targeted the same audience of first run cinemas. (264)

Martino's response suggests two issues with understanding *giallo* films in terms of the vernacular cinema paradigm: first, he makes clear that many *giallo* directors strove to make financially viable films that would be shown at first-run cinemas; second, he reminds us that many *giallo* films, including his own, were in fact shown in first-run cinemas. In fact, more recent scholarship has shown that cinematic *giallo* was very much a mainstream phenomenon in Italy throughout the 1960s and 1970s. Based on archival research of marketing materials in the collections at the Centro Sperimentale di Cinematografia-Cineteca Nazionale in Rome, Andreas Ehrenreich has found that the genre was generally well-represented in the programs of first-run cinemas, especially in the early 1970s (113). Ehrenreich reports that in the season between 1970 and 1971 *gialli* by Argento and Martino appeared on first-run bills, along with at least eight other examples of the genre by directors including Lucio Fulci, Luciano Ercoli, and Enzo Castallari (116–17), and he argues that assumptions about the exhibition and distribution of *giallo* films based on Wagstaff's reading of the Italian genre film industry "exaggerate the *giallo*'s marginality" (116).

This clarification is important because it reveals the complexity of the Italian *giallo* film's reception history; the *giallo* film was not always already a marginalized cultural artefact when English-language cult film audiences discovered it via video tape. The trajectory of the genre's canonization, or what Altman would call its "regenrefication," has not been linear. Before thinking through the genre's relation to the conditions of modernity, a mapping of its historically unstable cultural value will help us to understand and account for how the *giallo* has possessed multiple generic identities; it has been popular cinema, cult cinema, Italian cinema, and art cinema—sometimes simultaneously.

Tracing Regenrification: Home Video, *Giallo*, and the "Video Nasty" Phenomenon

If the inconsistent reception history of Argento's work traced by Russ Hunter is at all indicative of critical attitudes to *giallo* films more broadly, we must admit that any account of their regenrefication will begin in an imagined historical moment. That is to say, there is no truly stable situation from which such transformation suddenly begins; the *giallo* has always already meant many things. Nevertheless, the ripples of particular shifts coalesce and swell at certain points in time, registering a sense of movement in the critical consensus. We read this as a new wave of meaning that is itself always in flux. Let us turn back the clock to the mid-1970s, or the dawning of the home video age; a moment when technological innovation and changes in the distribution and exhibition of films combined to produce new ways of reading the *giallo* film.

The technical innovation that led to the wider availability of Italian and other global horror and exploitation cinemas emerged between 1975 and 1977, with Sony's Betamax released in 1975 in both Japan and the United States, closely followed by the 1976 Japan release and the 1977 United States release of JVC's rival format, VHS. Although the cost of both home video systems was initially prohibitively high, prices decreased steadily over the next three years and by 1980 home-video systems were becoming fixtures of the average household in developed countries. Despite the higher image resolution and stability initially offered by the Betamax system, the lower price of VHS recorders meant that JVC's technology claimed victory in the video tape war, becoming the premier format through which cult audiences could encounter Italian *giallo* films. And, as scholars such as Mark Levy have demonstrated, the impact home video had on the ways audiences consume and understand films is difficult to overstate. In light of more recent revolutions in distribution and exhibition—and the current near-extinction of the video store—it is important to revisit the particularity of this impact, which had a profound effect on the English-language reception of *giallo* films. The advent of home video meant that the encounter with films in the privacy of the domestic sphere was no longer limited to the curated selection available via television networks. With a video machine connected to your television, experiencing or revisiting films unlikely to be shown on television was suddenly made possible.

Despite its potential, major distributors displayed an initial reluctance to embrace this new medium that further threatened already declining box-office receipts; consequently, very few major film productions were released on video during this period. This led the early video market to become flooded with low-budget genre movies produced and distributed by small, independent film companies. Many of these films had enjoyed a theatrical release, but home video also became a way for film companies to distribute films refused certification for cinema release by governing bodies. Fanzines and magazines associated with video-collecting communities would later reflect on this early period of home video history as a kind of golden era of unregulated access to lower-budget horror films, older American and international horror and exploitation films, and movies with unchecked levels of graphic violence and sexual content. But while video buffs sat ensconced in their living rooms and bedrooms relishing the pleasures of these new levels of access, outside—in government and religious institutions and the conservative-leaning media—concern was growing about the private consumption of less-regulated "extreme" material.

The widespread panic surrounding the accessibility of violent and pornographic video tapes in the early 1980s was most visible in the United Kingdom, where the *Daily Mail* newspaper exploited these newly circulating fears by unleashing an orchestrated campaign specifically targeted at offensive video tapes. As Robert Fuoco points out, the *Daily Mail*'s campaign focused particularly on the harmful effects exposure to these films could have on Britain's youth and regularly cited their potential to cause psychological damage in articles such as "Rape of Our Children's Minds" (June 30, 1983). Their call for the government to "Ban the Sadist Videos" (February 25, 1983) spearheaded a moral crusade that led the Department of Public Prosecutions (DPP) to take action against the dissemination of apparently harmful video tapes. With no useful guidelines on content in place to organize prosecution of "sadist videos," in 1983 the DPP published a list of film titles that had been successfully prosecuted or against which it had filed charges. The films on this infamous list came to be known to the media and authorities as the "video nasties," a term coined by *Sunday Times* journalist Peter Chippendale in 1982 ("High Street Horror"). As video nasties historian Kate Egan outlines, after police raids and seizures there were some prosecutions, but the lack of official classification guidelines meant that many listed films could not be found guilty under the outdated 1959 Obscene Publications Act (*Trash or Treasure?*). To satiate this rapidly building moral panic incited by the media, in 1984 the Video Recordings Act was passed, incorporating markedly stricter censorship guidelines for video classification than for theatrical releases, reflecting the generalized concern that consumption of violent films was most problematic when it occurred in the privacy of the home.

Relatively few *giallo* films were officially targeted by the DPP, but the "Section 2" list made public in 1983 included Argento's 1982 film *Tenebrae*, which was successfully prosecuted but released in a heavily censored cut, as well as Mario Bava's final contribution to the *giallo* cycle, the quasi-*giallo* slasher *A Bay of Blood* (1971), which was refused classification for theatrical release in 1972. A censored cut of Bava's film was finally released in 1994. Alongside these *giallo* films, the second instalment of Argento's *Three Mothers* trilogy, *Inferno* (1980), also appeared, along with feature films such as *The Beyond* (1981) and *Cannibal Ferox* (1981) by renowned *giallo* directors Lucio Fulci and Umberto Lenzi respectively. The fact that Italian filmmakers were remarkably well represented overall was also problematic; prosecuted films by Italian directors included Ruggero Deodato's *Cannibal Holocaust* (1980) and Antonio Margheriti's *Cannibal Apocalypse* (1980); Giulio Berruti's nunsploitation film from 1979, *Killer Nun*; and Sergio Garrone's *SS Experiment Camp* (1976), whose agitative promotional artwork featured an illustration of a crucified topless woman hanging upside down within the walls of a concentration camp. At one point or another, thirty-three Italian productions or coproductions were officially listed, tying the reputation of Italian horror inextricably to this moral panic in English-speaking reception cultures.

Figure 2.1. VHS cover sleeve of Fletcher Video's precertification release of Dario Argento's *Deep Red* (1975), rated X. Digital scan.

More evidence of the demonization of Italian horror video in English-language contexts surfaced in 2010 when filmmaker Jake West's research led him to discover a DPP document containing a supplementary list of 82 additional film titles. Now known as the "Section 3" list, this document was never made public and features films that were unable to be prosecuted according to the Obscene Publications Act, but were nevertheless liable to seizure and confiscation from owners during police raids. This supplementary list includes Dario Argento's seminal *giallo Deep Red* (1975), as well as his supernatural masterpiece *Suspiria* (1977), alongside Marino Girolami's *Zombie Holocaust* (1980) and Deodato's *Last Cannibal World* (1977). The "Section 3" list suggests that VHS copies of *Deep Red* as well as the films of a host of other Italian exploitation cinema directors were regularly confiscated from UK collectors' homes during this time, cementing the status of Italian horror videotapes as contraband objects containing harmful foreign content.

The historical moment of the "video nasties" plays a significant role the *giallo*'s reception trajectory; as film historian Kim Newman writes, "Though the strict definition of a video nasty requires that it have made an appearance on the [official] DPP list, usage of the term has persisted well beyond the demise of the list" (135). This persistence to characterize particular films through the lens of this historical moment plays out across both time and space. Although Egan's study of the video nasties situates the debacle firmly in the nationally specific political context of Britain under the Thatcher government, the impact of this moral panic transcends both national and generic borders in that the controversy generated by this incident gave rise to a new way of talking about these films that pivots on their perceived *illegitimacy*. Italian horror's characterization as particularly nasty emerges in both marketing and audience response in the United States and Australia not long afterwards.

Egan recognizes two significant developments that emerge from this historical phenomenon and that are particularly relevant to this discussion of the *giallo* genre. Firstly, she sees the video nasties moral panic as a moment that effectively reconfigured the "context of origin" of relevant film titles by "collapsing their previous and distinct production and exhibition histories and reconfiguring their historical origin as an entirely video-based one in a contemporary UK cultural climate" ("Celebration" 204). Secondly, Egan sees the limited availability of these video titles as having acted as a catalyst for the generation of a particular taste culture built around a penchant for forbidden films—a culture whose "principle of organization" pivots on the DPP listing of banned videotapes. While titles confiscated in the UK may have become more and more rare, media coverage of the moral panic provided international distributors with a focused marketing strategy to respond to the rising demand for forbidden content. Films with provocative titles or particularly graphic cover art could be easily associated with this sense of danger despite never having appeared on the DPP's published list. In Australia for instance, where initial panic around availability of video tapes in the 1980s was most prevalent in Queensland, VHS distributors in other states used "Banned in Queensland!" stickers to attract buyer and renter attention to videotape titles including Argento's 1987 *giallo* film *Opera*. In the case of *Deep Red*, distributors of video releases of the film used strategies anchored in this moral panic to market full, "uncut" versions of the film to video audiences. The tags "uncut," "uncensored," and "finally available uncut!" appear on cover art for almost every video release of the film, and this discourse of rarity and exclusivity is evident even in post-2000 releases of the film, with the Umbrella 2004 release explicitly advertising the "uncut" status of its version on the cover of the DVD.

Altman describes this reprocessing of genre as "regenrefication," and he makes two excellent points about its process: first, that "family resemblances" across various films do not only occur in relation to intratextual filmic elements; rather, these codifying patterns also emerge through exhibition, marketing, and audiences (*Film/Genre* 98). Thus, it is not only the official members of the video nasties "family" that are impacted by its associated moral panic, but also films with "family resemblances." Second, Altman observes that "genres . . . are heavily dependent on the purposes of those who name, package, store, serve or consume them" (98). The reception history of *giallo* films in English-language markets has been irrefutably shaped by their status as *illegitimate* texts, and their recurrent marginalization has positioned them for adoption by audiences who see themselves as participants in oppositional taste cultures.

Paracinema

In his taxonomy of independent film publications dedicated to horror and exploitation cinema, David Sanjek makes a distinction between "fanzines" and "prozines"; while "fanzine" describes an amateur publication, "prozines" describe independent, commercially produced publications such as *Cinefantastique* (1970–) and *Fangoria* (1979–). Within the subgroup of horror fanzines, Sanjek identifies subsets of taste formations and modes among the various publication titles; *Temple of Schlock*, *Exploitation Retrospect*, and *Gore Gazette*, for instance, trade on a particularly sarcastic tone that "is often laced with self-conscious misogyny, racism and sexism" (154). Others, such as *Subhuman*, *Trash Compactor*, *Cold Sweat*, and *Sheer Filth*, position themselves by "nihilistically [identifying] with repulsive imagery" (156). Despite their differences, these publications are united in their opposition to "mainstream" or "legitimate" film and film culture; collectively, they can be understood as both a home and outlet for the strain of cult cinema reception Jeffrey Sconce calls "paracinema" (1995). According to Sconce, (sub)genres that typically take root within the paracinema canon include lesser-known splatter and slasher cycle horror films, low-budget science fiction movies, teen sex comedies, and government hygiene films, alongside "just about every other historical manifestation of exploitation cinema from juvenile delinquency documentaries to soft-core pornography" (372). While some particular film texts and genres are closely associated with the phenomenon, paracinema might be best described as a reading strategy or interpretive filter that is fundamentally interested in ironic readings of "badfilm" texts. In Sconce's words, "Paracinema is . . . less a distinct group of films than a particular reading protocol, a counter-aesthetic turned subcultural sensibility devoted to all manner of cultural detritus" (372). In the wake of its association with the DPP's list of dangerous videotapes, the Italian *giallo* film might have seemed at home within this counteraesthetic of celebrated illegitimacy.

While Sconce's typical paracinematic text might be described as particularly inaccessible or technically bankrupt, since the publication of his seminal essay "Trashing the Academy" (in which he coined the term), the concept of paracinema has been expanded by other critics and scholars to become more inclusive. In the work of Joan Hawkins, for example, the paracinema community's tastes are broadened to include classic horror and science fiction films, as well as selected European art cinema titles that are also celebrated by "legitimate" film culture. It is within this broader definition of paracinema that the Italian *giallo* film surfaces; when Hawkins refers to Dario Argento as a "paracinematic auteur," she aligns his authorship with both the glorious ineptitude of Ed Wood and the subversive poeticism of Luis Buñuel (232). Hawkins's interpretation of the paracinema taste protocol is established through a reading of horror and cult film fanzines and their mail-order catalogues; here she finds alphabetical lists of film titles that make "no attempt to differentiate among genres or subgenres, high or low art" (4) and argues that this, consequently, "challenges our continuing assumptions about the binary opposition of prestige cinema (European art and avant-garde/experimental film) and popular culture" (3).

The link Hawkins draws between Argento and the paracinema phenomenon also stems, at least partly, from the director's relatively consistent presence in the pages of paracinema publications such as *Uncut*, *Cinefantastique*, and *Video Watchdog*, where the coverage of his oeuvre, and his authorial persona, ranges from celebratory to fanatical. Paracinema auteurs are an important fixture of this culture, and Sconce describes them as

> "auteurs" who are valued more as "eccentrics" than as artists, who work within the impoverished and clandestine production conditions typical of exploitation cinema. [Their] films deviate from Hollywood classicism not necessarily by artistic intentionality, but by the effects of material poverty and technical ineptitude. (385)

Figure 2.2. Uncut sexploitation, Charles Manson figurines and Italian horror on video: mail order advertisements on page 75 of *Psychotronic Video*, number 18, in 1994. Digital scan.

It is difficult, however, to reconcile the case of many *giallo* directors with these terms. The "impoverished and clandestine production conditions" from which paracinema auteurs supposedly emerge do not apply to many of the Italian directors who made *giallo* films. Argento in particular has been the recipient of substantial Italian and international funding for his work at many points in his career and has never been aligned with the kind of budget-conscious style of horror auteurs like Herschell Gordon Lewis, either in Italy or abroad. Like their films, *giallo* directors often do not sit easily within critically defined parameters.

As a director with a dedicated fan base, Argento is represented in paracinema publications not as a director of schlocky horror films, but as a horror maestro whose authorial presence is as coveted as the films themselves. More often than not, it is his technical innovation that is celebrated; questions in interviews with the director are geared towards revealing the inspiration and intricacies of an unusual shot or spectacular death. Interviews with the director are also highly prized in this material produced for and by fans, where the opportunity to pick the director's brain becomes an invaluable source of extra material and information. The prozine and fanzine editions in which these interviews appear are then collected alongside the videotapes themselves, fortifying the sense of rarity within this countercultural sensibility and its canon of auteurs. Argento's key role in the cult of the paracinema auteur is further demonstrated in his appearance in the horror comic book series *Profondo rosso*, where he features as an illustrated version of himself and his name is used as a brand to attract a specific subcultural niche of readers.

The other reason Argento's work fits more easily into Hawkins's expanded notion of paracinema is that her interpretation emphasizes the points where "elite" and "low" cinema become confused within this reading strategy. While Sconce alludes to this slipperiness, Hawkins's close and critical reading of paracinema mail-order catalogues demonstrates just how tenuous taste distinctions are, when explicitly trashy flicks are literally listed alongside crossover films and canonized European art cinema. She argues that these listings and their principles of organization effectively "erase the difference between what is considered 'trash' and what is considered 'art,' through a deliberate leveling of hierarchies and recasting of categories" (16). Hawkins's analysis of these listings points to the rigid binary at the heart of the paracinema audience's reading strategy and reveals that this paradigm exists always in and because of its opposition to "culturally significant" cinema. Considering themselves a "disruptive force in the cultural and intellectual marketplace," whose manifesto advocates the valorization of "all forms of cinematic 'trash,'" the paracinephile's canon takes shape in opposition to the taste formations of "an elite cadre" of critics and film scholars (382). In other words, the paracinema canon is legitimized by those it supposedly opposes.

Significantly, the paracinema community constructs itself not only in opposition to what it sees as "elite" film culture, but also—much like the academy—in opposition to mainstream commercial cinema and its audiences, too. Sconce explains that,

> as in the academic film community, the paracinematic audience recognizes Hollywood as an economic and artistic institution that represents not just a body of films, but a particular mode of film production and its accompanying signifying practices. Furthermore, the narrative form produced by this institution is seen as somehow "manipulative" and "repressive," and linked to dominant interests as a form of cultural coercion. (381)

But as Mark Jancovich argues, a sense of distinction from the "conformist mass of viewers" is fundamental in legitimizing both paracinematic *and* academic taste formations in that it allows "them to present their own favored films as defamiliarizations of the 'signifying practices' associated with the mainstream" (310). The battle to assert their "authenticity" and supremacy over the function-orientated, narrative-driven cinematic reading associated with mass culture is fought by both the paracinema audience and academia. In actuality, the "caustic rhetoric" of paracinema works only to reaffirm the imagined distinctions between elite and low cultures and to further endorse the illegitimacy of those texts it celebrates. Take, for instance, the contents page of *Video Watchdog* that quotes Pauline Kael's avowedly paracinematic declaration, "If you can't enjoy a really bad movie, then you don't truly love movies"; these films, as Leon Hunt has suggested of Italian horror and Argento's work in particular, are "aestheticized 'bad' object[s]" as they exist both in the discourse of paracinema and within what it views as legitimate film culture. As Jancovich notes, "none of this [celebration of failure and technical ineptitude] is designed to oppose 'Hollywood,' 'mainstream, commercial cinema' or 'good taste,' but rather to affirm it" (313).

The historical origin of the paracinematic aesthetic is an issue complicated by the countless genres or kinds of films one might find under the umbrella term, but to acknowledge this is to understand something about their complexity as texts. Jancovich notes that "Sconce even contradicts himself by failing to acknowledge the historical nature of paracinematic aesthetic, and by presenting the film texts associated with it as *inevitably* producing specific 'effects' regardless of the cultural competences and dispositions of specific viewers" (311). Just as the audiences of Koven's vernacular cinema cannot be thought as a homogenous mass with uniform attitudes to the *giallo* film, neither can those films celebrated by paracinephiles be read only as part of this oppositional structure. Made up of films from across the globe, produced at almost any point in cinema's history, films celebrated by paracinema audiences may not always have been "bad" or commercially unsuccessful films. Like the video nasties phenomenon, the paracinema reading strategy collapses the prior history and past audiences of the film text. Just as the activity of the genre critic attempts to hold still the perpetually shifting system of genre in order to define what that genre is, the paracinema paradigm freezes those films it subsumes into an oppositional structure. In both cases, what is overlooked is that genres are not ahistorical systems with homogenous audiences.

Jancovich suggests that the term "cult cinema" might be more productive for coming to terms with the restlessness of film types like Italian *giallo*, because, unlike the paracinema audience, "cult movie audiences do not share a single, and certainly not a uniformly oppositional, attitude towards legitimate culture." He points out that "even within a single publication, the sheer eclecticism of the films discussed means that they are not read in one coherent way, but through a number of different and contradictory strategies that are constantly slipping into one another" (314). Taking this into account, we might say that understanding the nonlinear shifts in the *giallo* genre's status and cultural value can be more productively thought of as a process of *cultification*.

Technological Regenrefication

The video nasties list helped to "establish . . . the primacy and importance of obtaining 'original' prerecord versions of particular precertificate titles" to guarantee the collector both the best quality and the most "politically authentic version of a banned title" (Egan, "Celebration" 204). However, as Egan argues, the purpose of this operation developed throughout the

1990s "into a focus on the historically authentic value" of these videotapes (204). What Egan describes here, in contrast to other key writings on video, is the possibility of the videotape itself being a historical object with a traceable history, collected in a style not dissimilar to that described by Walter Benjamin in his essay on book collecting, "Unpacking My Library" (*Illuminations*). But how did this change once *giallo* films began to turn up on DVD?

The appeal of the Italian horror videotape as a collector's item may have crystallized around its status as a "gore-object," but Raiford Guins sees this as the first of two distinct stages in the reception of Italian horror in the United States, noting that "the second period is distinguished by DVD's elevation to the preferred medium through which to experience Italian horror cinema" (17). On one level this is no surprise; the launch of digital versatile disc technology in 1997 instigated an enormous shift in how we watch films in the home. With the significantly higher image and sound quality that DVD offered (especially when matched with a high-definition, widescreen television and surround sound system), the gap between theatrical exhibition and home movie presentation suddenly did not seem as wide. As Klinger points out, DVD technology more closely "approximate[d] the theatrical experience, thereby altering a film less dramatically" than VHS did (*Beyond the Multiplex* 61). The format was also promoted as a vastly superior medium for the preservation of films. The replacement for the bulky black cassette which housed plastic spools of magnetic tape was a slim and lightweight disc, with the digital data stamped into the delicate mirrored underside. Despite their relative fragility, DVDs—unlike videocassettes—could be played time and time again without risking the reduction of picture and sound quality. While the magnetic tape in the videocassette degrades each time the tape is played, the integrity of the data on digital optical discs remains stable as long as the surface is undamaged. This longevity, along with the format's extra space for the inclusion of special features, positioned DVDs as consumer items customers were more likely to purchase, rather than rent. The simultaneous rise of online stores and shopping websites throughout the late 1990s was also key to the DVD market explosion; the light-weight discs could also be more easily shipped around the world at low cost to the consumer.

While the DVD represented a generally a more attractive format for film collectors than its predecessor, the videocassette, Klinger reminds us that the mass production and wide availability of films on DVD does not service the desires of all film collectors. She writes that this type of collecting would seem to hold little potential for pursuing the ultimate collector's commodity—the rare artefact. Scarcity of the precious collectible—an elusive first edition of a book or a 35mm print of a forgotten work by a noted director, for example—is a condition that appears to be sorely lacking in this context. (66)

With the right setup, rare films could be quickly and cheaply reproduced from other disks and even transferred from videocassette with minimal loss of quality. Illegally produced discs could be purchased in the online equivalent of fanzine mail-order catalogues—e-stores specializing in rare, exploitation, and trash films, such as Something Weird Video, or auction sites, such as eBay (launched as AuctionWeb in 1995), where fans could enter bidding wars for DVD-R copies of then-rare Italian *giallo* films like Giulio Questi's *Death Laid an Egg* (1968). For Klinger, the paracinema community represents a "'shadow' culture of collectors" who are more likely to read poor image quality on DVDs as a marker of authenticity (62); nevertheless, the unprecedented opportunity to view and own films that had previously been unavailable threatened to dismantle the sense of rarity that had come to characterize many cult texts—especially those that had been corrupted or taken out of circulation by censorship bodies.

Paradoxically, this enduring subcultural ideology that Jancovich sees as emerging from a desire to "produce and protect a sense of rarity and exclusivity" is precisely what has ensured DVD companies a ready and waiting audience for myriad cult film DVD rereleases, including a large range of Italian *giallo* titles (309). In order to preserve the sense of scarcity and collectibility that has long characterized many of these films, specialist DVD companies have engaged many of the same marketing strategies larger mainstream companies use to ensure the unique value of particular titles is "explicitly designated" (Klinger 60). This is easiest to trace in the designs of DVD cover art for releases of Argento's *giallo* films in particular, because of the sheer number of releases. VCI Home Video's 1999 release of *The Bird with the Crystal Plumage* badges itself as an "Uncut Widescreen Presentation" of the film, while Umbrella Entertainment (Australia)'s 2006 disc offers an "uncut uncensored widescreen edition." Meanwhile, Shock Entertainment's 2015 release designates the film's status through its branding as part of their Cinema Cult series. Argento's *giallo* of 1971 *Four Flies on Grey Velvet* also offers salient examples of marketing strategies that emphasize collectibility: the DVD cover of RYKO Distribution (USA)'s 2009 release presents "Dario Argento's

LOST MOVIE, Full and Uncut," while Shameless Screen Entertainment (UK)'s 2012 DVD is branded as a "40th Anniversary Edition" of Argento's "Lost Masterpiece." As Klinger argues, marketing DVD titles in this way "provides an opportunity to elevate film to the status of high art, either by cashing in on an existing canon or by attempting to create one by affixing the 'classic' label" (*Beyond the Multiplex* 66). It is indeed via such marketing strategies that Argento's name began to be associated with the notion of the "classic," as on Umbrella Entertainment's three-disc *giallo* compilation package released in 2007 under the title *Argento Classics*.

Figure 2.3. Lost masterpiece recovered: cover art for a 2012 release of Dario Argento's *Four Flies on Grey Velvet* (1971) from Shameless Screen Entertainment.

The multiple releases of key *giallo* films since the late 1990s demonstrates that cultists and *giallo* fans will buy multiple copies of the same titles if a new release offers valuable supplementary material in the form of disc "extras" or significant improvement to image or sound quality. This is partly due to the increasing prominence of what Klinger calls the "hardware aesthetic," or a mode of film reception that "conceives of value according to imperatives drawn from technological considerations" and through which "a film's worth is judged by the quality of the transfer, the aura of the digital reproduction of sound and image, and even the pristine surface of the disc itself" (*Beyond the Multiplex* 75–76). As home theater systems and high-definition televisions became more sophisticated and more affordable, tech-savvy consumers could expect to experience something closer to the spectacle of theatrical exhibition within the comfort of their own homes, and thus increasingly sought out films types and genres, such as those heavy on special effects, that showcase high-definition image capabilities and sophisticated sound systems. Klinger argues that this new technophile-spectatorship has the power to effectively reconfigure the prior status of films by "rereading . . . films through the ideology of the spectacular" and representing the "triumph of a particular notion of form over content" (*Beyond the Multiplex* 75).

While Klinger's point is that this demand for spectacle has the power to strip classical Hollywood and foreign cinema of "canonical status," the Italian *giallo* film represents one set of historical foreign films whose canonization the hardware aesthetic has only further crystallized. In the first instance, the formal experimentation and excessively violent set-pieces associated with the most well-known *giallo* films and directors fulfils the technophile's demand for spectacle. But because the *giallo*'s reception history has coded the genre in terms of scarcity and illegitimacy, *giallo* fans and cultists are also implicated in an ongoing struggle to "restore" *giallo* films via these technologies. There are a range of online sites that house this discourse, but the *giallo* entries on review website DVD Beaver (www.dvdbeaver.com) offer a salient example of this dedication to uncovering the very best version of particular films. Close to one hundred Italian *giallo* titles are reviewed here, along with films that are sometimes "mid-identified as giallo" and a range of English and non-English language films that are influenced or related to *giallo* films in some way. These reviews place particular emphasis on the technical specifications and digital standards of the releases they cover. The page for Bava's *Blood and Black Lace*, for instance, includes a plot summary; stills of the film's various titles as they appear in different cuts of the film; a compilation of original promotional poster artwork; cover artwork and image and sound specifications (including bitrate charts) for various DVD and Blu-ray releases arranged in a comparative table; and a detailed series of screen captures of identical frames from each release that allow the reader to compare (and purchase) the available circulating versions. *Giallo* films have thus benefitted from the prioritization of "digital standards of excellence" that Barbara Klinger sees DVD technology to have ushered in, even if this has configured their value principally in terms of spectacle (*Beyond the Multiplex* 77).

Additionally, while the introduction of DVD clearly changed the parameters for consumption of *giallo* films and other marginalized media, it is important to note that these shifts were neither linear nor ubiquitous; as Sexton points out, the seeds of Italian horror's "remediation" as art were sown by cult film enthusiasts and videotape collectors well before the arrival of DVD (21). And, as Church has shown, this "remaking" has not followed "a teleological path toward increased cultural value" (15–16). For every uncut collector's edition of Argento's *Deep Red* in circulation there is a more easily accessible, low-quality release floating in budget bins in DVD superstores.

In the face of this constellation of meanings and contradictory positions, the most recent rereleases of *giallo* films on Blu-ray have continued to emphasize image and sound quality through the "special edition" marketing device, whilst both expanding the canon of "quality" *giallo* and further contextualising the films as those worthy of scholarly analysis. Writing on the DVD, Klinger points out that the notion of the "expandable text" has become so important to establishing a film's collectibility for the home market that filming and recording supplementary material is built into the production process on new projects (*Beyond the Multiplex* 72). But for rereleases of older films, supplementary material must be compiled retrospectively, from residual archival material or new content that takes a retrospective approach. If, as Klinger argues, "the special edition trades off the revelation as key ingredient of its appeal," (*Beyond the Multiplex* 72) what revelations are offered by *giallo* rereleases on Blu-ray?

Arrow Video's 2018 release of *The Bird with the Crystal Plumage*, for instance, delivers a 4k restoration produced from the original negative, offered in high-definition Blu-ray (1080p) presentation. The revelation delivered does not relate only to a new level of image clarity, but to vast improvements in the color grading, making skin tones warmer and colors generally richer. For Gary Tooze at DVD Beaver, this has a direct bearing on the film's relationship to the *giallo* genre. In his comparative reviews of various releases of Argento's film he writes that "some individuals will endlessly debate about the authenticity of a Blu-ray image but I can only tell you this looks stunningly beautiful. Colors are so rich and _Giallo_-esque—looking opulent, evoking baroque or rococo—intense, stylistic but never embellished" (review of *Bird with Crystal Plumage*). Likewise, their 2019 "special edition" Blu-ray of Luigi Bazzoni's *The Fifth Cord* is advertised as a "brand new 2K restoration produced from the original camera negative," which, according to Tooze, produces "colors, contrast, detail [that] are all far in advance of the bland DVD image. . . . It looks textured and the colors have depth and vibrancy." He adds that "Arrow are doing some amazing work in the Giallo genre," which is conceived of as a long-term, ongoing project of restoration (review of *The Fifth Cord*).

If the image and sound specifications satisfy the ever-rising standards of the hardware aesthetic, the supplementary material included in each release is designed to appeal to the film collector's specialist knowledge of these cult films. Argento's film is accompanied by a new interview with the director himself, as well as interviews with selected actors. Similarly, the Blu-ray release of Bazzoni's film includes interviews with actor Franco Nero and the film's editor Eugenio Alabiso, along with a previously unseen sequence that had not made it into the final cut for original theatrical release. Each of these inclusions are part of what Klinger sees as strategized product differentiation that enables DVD companies and distributors to resell titles they have often already released. This does not simply lift the status of the films, but for Klinger results in "an instant built-in and changeable intertextual surround that enters into [the film's] meaning and significance for viewers" (*Beyond the Multiplex* 72).

What distinguishes the intertextual surround of recent *giallo* rereleases on Blu-ray from other manifestations of "specialized" film-fan knowledge is the scholarly emphasis that emerges in their supplementary material. Alongside cast and crew interviews, Arrow Video include commissioned visual essays and other forms of scholarly analysis that takes the expandability of the films in the direction popularized by Janus Films' Criterion Collection. An illustrative example can be found in the special features of the 2019 rerelease of *The Bird with the Crystal Plumage*, which includes a visual essay titled "The Power of Perception" by scholar Alexandra Heller-Nicholas, whose sophisticated analysis of the film counters "reductive declarations" about the roles of gender, violence, and perception in Argento's work. In this respect then, premium Blu-ray rereleases of *giallo* films do continue the process of remediation described by Guins, except that the films' marginalized status and obscured cultural value is both unpacked and reiterated via this specialized, scholarly supplementary material. If, as Klinger argues, "collected objects ultimately refer to the collector as a kind of auteur, a producer of an intelligible, meaningful, private cosmos," the *giallo*'s cult canonization, via the activity of these collectors, carries the capital of its illegitimate past (*Beyond the Multiplex* 89).

Organized and displayed on shelves like books, *giallo* films on DVD and Blu-ray embody the transformation of films as "public objects into home furnishings that respond to the concerns and rituals of domestic space" (*Beyond the Multiplex* 57). But there is another type of highly aestheticized ancillary *giallo* text currently experiencing a surge in popularity amongst collectors: the *giallo* soundtrack vinyl rerelease. While *giallo* soundtracks have, like the films themselves, long been sought-after objects for cult collectors, the vinyl market's recent surge in growth has propelled demand for rereleases and compilations of previously obscure Italian soundtrack material. For casual genre fans familiar with films by Argento, the *giallo* soundtrack might be characterized by the protracted compositions of Italian prog-rock band Goblin who scored his most well-known films *Deep Red* and *Suspiria*. Indeed, renewed interest in Argento's work prompted the reformation of the group, and, since 2014, they have toured extensively, playing complete scores live for screenings of Argento's films to international audiences. But scores for *giallo* films were often written by renowned Italian composers, including Ennio Morricone, Riz Ortolani, and Bruno Nicolai, and were an important site of musical experimentation. Director Peter Strickland describes the *giallo* score's influence on his own film, the neo-*giallo* of 2012, *Berberian Sound Studio*:

> I thought about the stories behind some of the *giallo* soundtracks; they were very advanced for the time with their use of drone, *mystique concrete*, free jazz and dissonance. The music of Bruno Maderna, Ennio Morricone and Gruppo di Improvisazione Nuova Consonanza existed in the same high art camp as Stockhausen, Cage, or AMM, but then these guys were making money on the side composing soundtracks for B-grade horror films. *Berberian Sound Studio* came out of that strange, sonic no-man's-land between academia and exploitation. (Jason Wood 133)

This point "between academia and exploitation" where Strickland positions the *giallo* score has garnered increased visibility through the recent surge the in popularity of film soundtracks amongst vinyl record collectors. In his study of cult film soundtracks and the vinyl boom, Sexton notes collectors' particular interest in "soundtracks which stem form a number of exploitation or more obscure arts films made between the 1960s and early 1980s," which a number of record companies currently focus on servicing (13). UK-based label Death Waltz Recording Company have released a number of these sought-after *giallo* titles, including Bruno Nicolai's hauntingly cool score for Sergio Martino's 1971 film *The Case of the Scorpion's Tail*, described on the Death Waltz website as "a soundtrack enthusiast's wet dream."

Figure 2.4. Death Waltz Recording Company's 2017 vinyl release of composer Bruno Nicolai's lush score for *The Case of the Scorpion's Tail* (Sergio Martino, 1971). Digital scan.

While the attention to design and overall quality of Death Waltz's *giallo* records would appear to rhyme with the "hardware aesthetic" of Blu-ray rereleases, these vinyl rereleases of *giallo* scores use subtly different strategies to pitch to audiophile consumer-collectors. Artwork for *The Case of the Scorpion's Tail* references the pulpy covers of Mondadori's literary *gialli*, with a circular composition of images from the film that drips blood into the bright yellow border. The artwork and layout of the expansive gatefold sleeve is attributed to artist Eric Adrian Lee and encases two 180 gram vinyl records as well as a reproduction of the original Italian playbill poster, which literally enables fans to furnish their home with a replica of this once-public object. What makes the pressing particularly distinctive—and highly collectible—however, is the fact that the records themselves are pressed in a combination of red, yellow, and black wax, producing a highly polished, abstracted simulacrum of the *giallo* genre's characteristic color palette. Sexton notes that the packaging of records has played an important role in the vinyl revival by helping to foreground the status of the format as an analogue technology with a "cultish aura" (17). If digital technologies have increased the accessibility to Italian *giallo* films, the *giallo* soundtrack on vinyl returns the genre to its predigital roots, albeit via a marketing strategy that emphazises its sense of retro cool.

In a discussion about the critical notion of a new cinephilia, Adrian Martin responds to his coauthors by writing that "video-buff culture can sometimes be a strange, nerdish, exasperating, and disappointingly limited thing, but I don't think it is a bad thing, because it has opened up new intensities, new streams for the circulation and appreciation of cinema" (Martin and Rosenbaum 43). This is a productive way to think about the reception trajectory of the *giallo*. While the often limiting nature of strategies like Sconce's paracinema is retrospectively clear, we might see them as fundamental developments along the trajectory of *giallo* cinema's regenrification; integral detours the genre has undertaken on its road to becoming a legitimate cult(ural) product. Such audiences have represented for video companies an established audience of fans and collectors whose drive to complete and restore the canon has resulted in its fortifications and expansion. Guins suggests that "Italian horror films on DVD mark an attempt to repair the low status (and low quality) afforded their initial presence on videocassette as well as an effort to exchange the 'sophomoric' fanzine nomenclature that over-determined the object during its initial mass mediation" (25).

But while the technologies of DVD and Blu-ray, along with the proliferation of online marketplaces, have played an undeniably important role in the regenrefication of genres like the *giallo*, as Sexton points out, music cultures also actively contribute to the shifting values ascribed to older films, and technologies alone are not responsible for the new visibility of these historically marginalized films (13). Clutching their videotapes (and then their discs), these cult audiences of cinephile/technophile collectors carved a history of critical response that established the *giallo*'s textual conventions, motifs, and themes, helping future audiences to recognize embedded patterns of meaning.

The *giallo* grows increasingly visible as a critically legitimate cinema: in 2012 and 2013 Anthology Film Archives in New York presented "Giallo Fever!" screening programs. In 2018 the Gallery of Modern Art in Queensland, Australia, ran a retrospective season of Italian horror titled "Gothic, Giallo, Gore: Masters of Italian Horror," which featured films by Argento, Bava and Fulci; in partnership with the gallery, Australian gelato institution Messina developed the "Smooth Criminal"—a *giallo*-themed chocolate gelato bar to consume between disorientating zooms and blood-curdling screams.

3

No Place like Home

The Late-Modern City

> One sees thus once again that a grand hotel is a world unto itself, and this world resembles the rest of the big world.
>
> —Sven Elvestad, *Death Enters the Hotel*

❧

THE FIRST SHOT OF GIULIANO Carnimeo's *The Case of the Bloody Iris* (1972) is a close-up: a woman wearing red nail polish drops a coin into the slot of a public telephone and picks up the receiver. The voice on the other end of the line instructs her to "come up," and she steps out of the glassed-in silence of the telephone booth onto the busy streets of Rome, with Bruno Nicolai's bittersweet jazz theme and the film's opening credits punctuating her commute. She enters a lobby busy with people in coats and hats, and, as she jostles her way to the front of the elevator queue, the film's score falls away. Inside the full compartment, people with blank stares stand close to one another, unmoved neither by their proximity to others nor the inconvenience. In the silence, time moves slowly. The bodies of the elevator's occupants are fragmented in close-up shots: a hand, an ear, a nose. The woman glances at her fellow travelers, but her gaze is not returned. In this small space, densely packed with unresponsive individuals, the woman cannot notice that her killer is in the lift, too. The elevator ascends and begins to empty, depositing people at their respective floors, while the faceless figure in the corner pulls on thick latex gloves. And, finally, when they are the only two people in the lift, the killer covers her mouth and, in a series of rapidly edited close-ups, stabs her with a small knife and her sticky paint-like blood hemorrhages through the lilac wool of her suit. The killer flees and the woman is left lying on the floor, waiting to be discovered by unsuspecting, shocked, and concerned passengers.

These people she waits for never really arrive. Instead, when the doors open at the top level, three residents are caught off-guard by the grisly scene. An initial moment of shock, obligatory and rehearsed, quickly gives way to concerns about who the victim might be and how this incident might interfere with their daily routines. Seconds after the gruesome discovery—completely recovered and slightly miffed at the inconvenience—the youngest of the three, a nightclub dancer, announces she must dash to make her rehearsal on time. Like the passengers in the elevator, these inhabitants of the late-modern city cannot see how the space they inhabit might position them as members of a community; they cannot participate in this space as eyewitnesses or as neighbors.

It is no accident that many of the spaces the *giallo* film's characters and audience experience recall Kracauer's description of the hotel lobby, a place where "togetherness . . . has no meaning" ("The Hotel Lobby" 184). As an architect, philosopher, and cultural critic who wrote extensively on the conditions of life in the first part of the twentieth century, Kracauer was keenly interested in the detective novel and what it had to say about modernity; in its original form, "The Hotel Lobby" was part of a book-length study of the detective novel he wrote between 1922 and 1925. In this essay, Kracauer argues that the hotel lobby is the definitive locale of the modern detective novel: a place characterized by anonymity and disconnection, exemplifying the conditions of modernity. Kracauer compares the characteristics of the hotel lobby—a space in which transient and drifting individuals find themselves—to those of the church, that place where a community congregates to worship en masse. In each case, spatial experience is characterized by its difference to our relationship to space in everyday life; unlike the sense of community fostered by the practice of group worship in the church, however, in the quintessentially modern space of the hotel lobby, the experience of detachment from everyday life has no purpose. Those who inhabit the hotel lobby are, as Anthony Vidler describes, "scattered like atoms in a void, confronted with 'nothing' " (72), connected only by their anonymity.

In the opening sequence of Carnimeo's film, the milieu of modernity that Kracauer and Vidler describe is folded up and packed into the apartment block's elevator.

While the generic conventions of the *giallo* guide the film's narrative along a predetermined course, the film's editing works to foreground the tropes of disassociation, fragmentation, and isolation that Kracauer sees at work in the hotel lobby. And this "world unto itself," is, for Kracauer, a space that "resembles the rest of the big [modern] world" ("The Hotel Lobby" 184). If a detailed analysis of the elevator scene in *The Case of the Bloody Iris* reveals it as a small-scale manifestation of the hotel lobby scenario, an abrupt zoom out exposes a world redolent of the sticky ink of fresh newspapers, polishing balm on leather armchairs, and the crispness of freshly starched collars—or their late-modern equivalents. The *giallo* genre behaves like a glass prism that refracts the milieu of Kracauer's hotel lobby, pulls it through time and disperses it as an entire world.

In this space that Vidler describes as a "void," the impossibility of meaningful experience or exchange between its inhabitants is symptomatic of the ambiguity that so often undermines and eclipses the narrative logic of *giallo* films. As we see with the uninterested neighbors who discover the dead body in their elevator, this curious existence is characterized by an uneasy relation to the suspense and horror of typical narratives of detection; despite their circumstances, the *giallo*'s characters live as if they are "confronted with nothing" (Vidler 72). The four films discussed in this chapter—*The Fifth Cord* (Luigi Bazzoni, 1971), *The Black Belly of the Tarantula* (Paolo Cavara, 1971), *The Case of the Bloody Iris*, and *Tenebrae* (Dario Argento, 1982)—each offer doors into this ambiguous space where human existence mimics that of the "ungraspable flat ghosts" Kracauer describes ("The Hotel Lobby" 183). The hotel lobby's "coming and going of unfamiliar people" (183) is replayed in the perpetual flux of arrivals and departures and in the inconsequentiality of violence carried out in the *giallo* city. These are characteristics of a world where nothing is stable, knowable, finite, or fixed: people catch late flights, ascend and descend staircases, and disappear into cabs that speed away into the distance. Or they spend the afternoon in the countryside rehearsing the tired conventions of the romantic tryst, before returning to cold, grey, urban centers to run down anonymous hallways or across the tops of buildings of some architectural interest. One girl gets murdered, another moves into her apartment; a single line of dialogue begins in a car and ends in a park. As Franco Nero's character Andrea Bild tells the chief investigator in *The Fifth Cord*, "They're coming and going all the time, from all over the world. It's like a hotel."

Figure 3.1. Journalist Andrea (Franco Nero) descends one of many spiral staircases in Luigi Bazzoni's *The Fifth Cord* (1971). Digital frame enlargement.

A number of *gialli* are set in the countryside, but, unsurprisingly, the late-modern city is the key locale for many of these Italian crime films. And while some *gialli* juxtapose the over-represented classical city with indistinguishable modern locales, many of the films do away entirely with recognizable settings like Rome's Piazza di Spagna and the Fontana di Trevi. The dispersal of place and the bleak reflection of urban sprawl in the *gialli* discussed here refuse their characters the security of a stable or meaningful position from which to orient themselves. In this group of films, the cityscape and its architecture work to fragment identities, to hinder communication between individuals, and to lend their dark recesses only to the playing out of a highly aestheticized violence. Here, the city is an anonymous, uncertain, and unfathomable space, where the energy of modernity's tension has given way to a pervasive anxiety that heralds the period's collapse.

Sustained investigation of the fragmented and decentered *giallo* city forces us to confront a space that lies between the two points of Frederic Jameson's distinction "between modernism's experience of existential time and deep memory and postmodernism's discontinuous spatial experience" (quoted in Friedberg 171). This is not, however, a moment adequately described by theory that positions high modernist films as pre-postmodern, for such theoretical frameworks fail to account for the peculiar tonality of the *giallo* world: a tonality that laments the passing of grand narratives it cannot quite remember, in a world unable to shift gear or move forward. These films operate in and around a moment characterized not by nostalgia or utopian ambition (failed or otherwise), but by a kind of decadent dementia. Thus, rather than (pre-)postmodern, we might consider the *giallo* film as an exemplar of *late-modern* cinema: a cinema in conscious and reflexive dialogue with the particular conditions of late modernity.

Running Through Centrifugal Space and the Architectural Imaginary

We can move towards understanding the dynamics of the *giallo*'s cities through considering the two descriptions of city space that Edward Dimendberg employs in his analysis of the Hollywood film noir city: "centripetal" and "centrifugal." The terms are employed in a more expansive sense than that typically used by architects and geographers, in that here they describe not only the actual built environment but also "the range of attitudes, behaviors, and shared interpretations that crystallize around it" (99). Centripetal describes a force of curvature; like water disappearing down a plughole, centripetal force moves a body towards a center. Centripetal space thus articulates a spatial organization whose density is concentrated at its center. Engaging with this articulation of the city, a film might exhibit "a fascination with urban density and the visible—the skyline, monuments, recognisable public spaces, and inner-city neighbourhoods" (177). Conversely, the tendency towards centrifugal configurations is expressed via the widespread expansion of urban spaces, the building of shopping malls and new industrial landscapes and highways. Dimendberg explains that

> characteristics of centrifugal space include the decreased significance of metropolitan density and agglomeration and their replacement by dispersed settlements and a shift from urban verticality to the horizontal sprawl of suburbs and larger territorial units. But one might also discern centrifugal space in the redeployment of surveillance mechanisms away from the body of city dwellers toward the automobile, the proliferation of electronic media, and the collection of traffic statistics as a strategy of control. (92)

By establishing this distinction between centrifugal and centripetal space, Dimendberg shows how these Hollywood crime films map the conditions and development of American city space during this period, chronicling a shift from conceptions of the modern city as a recognizable center where monuments and skyscrapers etch dramatic lines in the sky, to the flattened, sprawling highways and suburbs of late modernity. Like a number of the film noirs Dimendberg discusses, Italian *giallo* films such as *The Girl Who Knew Too Much* and *Who Saw Her Die?* (Aldo Lado, 1972) exhibit a tendency to oscillate between these two spatial organizations, using the juxtaposition to produce a sense of instability and uncertainty. But, unlike those films, *The Case of the Bloody Iris*, *The Fifth Cord*, *The Black Belly of the Tarantula*, and *Tenebrae* draw more heavily on the centrifugal configurations Dimendberg associates with the postwar period.

At a micro level, the description of this shift from a prominence of verticality (the tower, the monument) in the prewar city to a focus on horizontal sprawl (the suburb, the factory) in the postwar period can be used as a starting point for describing space in *giallo* films like *The Fifth Cord*, where action occurs chiefly in factories, apartment buildings, and tunnels, rather than in a recognizable city center. From a macro perspective, this conceptualization of changing representations of space is useful in the case of the *giallo* for at least two reasons. Firstly, the Italian genre's relationship to the film noir of classical Hollywood, as noted by scholars like Mary P. Wood, suggests some interesting comparisons of the way each uses space and the cityscape. Dimendberg observes, for instance, how the evocation of the American city as a place of fear and isolation in film noir suggests a distinct break between the critical concepts of pre- and postwar modernity, while the utopian ideal aligned with the historical avant-garde movements of the 1920s (early modernism) has, post-1945, been subsumed by an evocation of the city that is cold and troubled. He explains that

> film noir deployed the representational strategies of avant-garde photography or modernist painting at the service of an aesthetic transfiguration *without* social transcendence. The metropolis portrayed in the film noir cycle seldom appears defamiliarized or re-enchanted, a space of genuinely enhanced freedom and possibility, but emerges instead as a highly rationalized and alienating system of exploitative drudgery permitting few possibilities of escape. ("From Berlin to Bunker Hill" 65)

This rationalized and alienating noir city could be the setting for any of the *giallo* films discussed here, because their global modern city aesthetic that could be any place lends a sense of vague familiarity. The formal treatment of characters' experiences in the transient and fragmented *giallo* city also resonates with Dimendberg's observation about the ways the film noir's aesthetic utilizes representational strategies of modernism without subscribing to the utopian modernist program of transcendence through art. The final chapter of this book explores the *giallo* genre's relationship with modernism in greater detail.

The opening sequence of *The Case of the Bloody Iris* begins to demonstrate already this tendency to paint the organization of city space in a configuration that seems to spiral outwards; its montage of street-level shots of crowded streets obscures the recognition of specific places, foregrounding instead the chaos of the modern metropolis. Such montage sequences are typical of the opening credit sequences in *giallo* films, but the centrifugal configuration of city space is reiterated across the duration of the films too, through a range of recurrent motifs and formal patterns. One such pattern is the chase sequence, which frequently foregrounds the city's horizontal lines and modernist architecture through characters' negotiation of this space. The *giallo* chase sequence is experienced both as a typical action set piece and as a late-modern tour of the lowlights of the city's postwar expansion: suspects are pursued through run-down industrial parks, abandoned office buildings, and warehouses with broken windows. Such chase sequences rarely provide closure to the narrative events out of which they arise; recalling Barbara Klinger's description of what she calls "progressive genres," *giallo* films routinely "refuse closure" of their overall narratives, as well as of plot incidents ("Cinema/Ideology/Criticism").

The Black Belly of the Tarantula offers a salient example of this refusal when protagonist Inspector Torrini (Giancarlo Giannini) attempts to apprehend two possible suspects engaged in a game of cat and mouse playing out in and around an abandoned modernist office block, fenced by a robust gate. Torrini arrives at the scene and the film, propelled by a shift in the soundtrack to Morricone's frenetic jazz score, cuts to a skewed-angle shot of the dwarfed suspects running out onto the enormous rooftop. Back on the ground, the security gate and booth are abandoned, so Torrini scales the fence to gain access to the block. The film shifts abruptly once more to a low-angled shot, framing the suspects as they traverse the multileveled rooftop. Next, the camera is back on the street, tracking a red sports car pulling up at the site. The driver's face is obscured, but the recurrent *giallo* motifs of black gloves and dark hat mark this driver as another possible suspect. The presence of a third party traversing this already difficult space introduces a new level of complexity to the detection narrative, but within the context of the chase sequence it also multiplies the possibilities of fragmentation and disorientation.

In a medium shot, Torrini scrambles up an external spiral staircase in an attempt to reach the suspects on the roof, who are chasing one another along the length of the enormous building. Our sense of perspective is then shattered by a rapid zoom out which reframes the staircase in its entirety, before shifting back to a medium shot to show Torrini finally reaching the roof. An extreme long shot reestablishes the situation unfolding on the building's rooftop against an overcast sky whose horizon is littered with the grey debris of industry. This assault of disorienting changes in perspective is amplified by Morricone's increasingly schizophrenic composition. The next vertigo-inducing shot from the roof looks down to trace the red car as it slowly circles the building, before the first point of view shot of its driver takes in the building at ground level with an eerie voyeurism. Back on the roof, the action moves closer towards the center of the building, where some inadequate railing borders a drop to an enclosed central courtyard. Torrini yells for the suspects to stop, but it is too late: the first falls into the center of the building, smashing office windows as he passes through the still air, before landing on the paving of the otherwise empty courtyard. His body lies still on the concrete, in a crime-scene configuration that offsets the perfect symmetry of the four walls of glass windows and their infinite reflection.

The remaining players resume their chase around the perimeter of the roof and a low-angled shot from the road shows how the red car continues to trace the circumference of the site at a slow, sinister pace. Mirroring this circular movement through space, the suspect runs back down the spiral staircase, his head disappearing and reappearing as he scrambles down its steps before scaling the outer fence and taking off down the street, with Torrini in close pursuit. The frenetic pace of the score reaches a crescendo as the red car pulls around behind Torrini in a close-up shot, momentarily obscuring the spectacle of the chase. An abrupt and disorienting shift across the axis of action heightens the chaotic tension further by repositioning the mysterious driver to suggest that the car will now pursue the two men who are on foot and it becomes clear that the driver, who is gaining on the detective and his original suspect, intends to knock one of them down. Realizing this, Torrini runs off to the right of frame while the car speeds up to follow the suspect who veers left of frame. As the car runs him off the road, we assume the point of view of the suspect as he falls to the ground—a chaotic jumble of industrial steel and tarmac—before the car speeds away. Morricone's score amplifies the strangeness of this moment by returning to the film's sensual opening theme, as Torrini rolls the suspect's body over in a shaky low-angled shot. He stares at the man's blood-covered face for a moment before pulling an indistinguishable clue from the victim. Raising his head to survey the empty street, Torrini sees nothing and no one, so he walks away from the crime scene, leaving the corpse in the middle of the road.

While the frenetic pace of the editing in this sequence is not unusual for action-oriented set pieces, the interplay between this and other formal choices produces sensations of profound disruption and instability. The camera's unnerving angles and unexpected shifts work against the principles of continuity, instead producing the sense of disorientation and chaos we find often in the *giallo* world. These highly stylized shots are juxtaposed with static shots of the built environment that the characters chase one another through, highlighting their isolation and foregrounding the inconsequentiality of violence, or its retribution, in these spaces of alienation. Characters move down or across the frame, but they never seem to reach anywhere significant before their world collapses around them in a violent end.

A similar chase sequence in *The Fifth Cord* ensues when journalist Andrea comes home to his apartment to discover a lurking intruder. Upon fleeing the apartment building, the stranger runs into a dark concrete tunnel illuminated by the sickly glow of a small fluorescent lamp. Andrea follows, and the pair come out the other side onto the street, arriving at an enormous abandoned and derelict concrete factory building. Inside, the gutted structure is filled with broken-down machinery that enhances the impression of isolation, but the industrial ceiling lamps uncannily swing to and fro, building tension and destabilizing the space, while simultaneously recalling the swinging lamps of the abandoned apartment Nora visits in *The Girl Who Knew Too Much*. Andrea and his assailant run into a series of empty hallways whose broken and grimy windows interact with the light from outside to throw stark compositional contrasts across the men's faces and surrounding walls. As they struggle against one another across the width of the hallway, the light in Vittorio Storaro's cinematography shifts from blue to white to blue again, magnifying the locale's disconnection from safe or recognizable space. As they shove one another against the dusty window panes, the glass breaks as if made from sugar, tinkling and echoing through the emptiness of space. The sense of disconnection and alienation is compounded by the relative lack of establishing shots and through the seemingly endless network of anonymous hallways. They encounter no one else, and no police turn up to restore order.

As in the examples above, this centrifugal tendency typically eschews architectural icons of the overrepresented city in favor of a markedly hegemonic, global architectural style. Mary P. Wood explains that Italy's cultural diversity lends itself particularly well to the expression of cultural climates or values in cinema, but notes in her writing on space, place, and the Italian crime film that "although classical architecture provides a recurring metaphor for an ordered, stable, coercive system of values, by far the most commonly evoked architectural style in 1970s conspiracy thrillers is that of the 1960s" (*Italian Cinema* 188). Instead, this globally recognizable style that Wood refers to is rooted in the modernist architecture brought to the world's attention by Henry-Russell Hitchcock and Philip Johnson in their 1932 exhibition and its accompanying book, *The International Style: Architecture since 1922*. Like any genre, the idea of the International Style is, as the authors attest in forewords for subsequent editions, a complex, shifting, and variable system based on principles of both repetition and difference. In their book, Hitchcock and Johnson espouse the defining characteristics of the style—the expression of volume rather than mass, balance rather than perceived symmetry and the rejection of applied ornament—with evangelical fervor, and the rigidity that the authors prescribe in the original edition make for a tone that Johnson himself in 1995 calls "preachy and schoolmarmish" (13). Nevertheless many of its key stylistic characteristics and principles are at play in the later 1960s examples of architecture that so often define the aesthetic of the *giallo* city. As Wood notes, the style is so prevalent in Italian crime films that an entire study could be devoted solely to the role of modern architecture in the *giallo* (*Italian Cinema* 188). Here the particular focus is on how the use of International Style architecture in the *giallo* so often subverts the style's utopian, functionalist ideologies.

While Hitchcock and Johnson's work focuses primarily on the aesthetic qualities of the International Style, the ideological foundations of many of its greatest examples have at their heart a dedication to a modern form of functionalism. For many of the architects associated with the style, including Le Corbusier, the process of design began always with an analysis of the building's function and of the best technical means of meeting it. Aesthetic character, instead of being superimposed, emerges as part of this process. It is precisely this principle that Le Corbusier refers to in his manifesto, *Toward an Architecture*, when he famously writes that "a house is a machine for living" (151). By the 1960s, the modern aesthetic that grew in the first half of the twentieth century from the idea that "the exterior is the result of an interior" (88), fulfilled the prophecy embedded in its name, becoming a global and truly international style. Writing in 1966, Hitchcock describes the International Style as "the lines that, after 1930, led to *our* present in the 1960s" (23). During the postwar economic boom in Italy, it was this architectural style that dominated new building and housing projects of the rapidly expanding cities. But the *giallo* film's framing of these spaces destabilizes the utopian functionality and livability of this modern aesthetic. In films like *The Fifth Cord*, office and apartment buildings are empty, or else their sheer size works to dwarf and isolate the individuals who run through them. Modernist homes—once machines for living—become in the *giallo* environments of perversion, violence, and murder.

Dimendberg describes the film noir city as an "apprehensive urban representation" ("Berlin to Bunker Hill" 65), and it is perhaps this that Koven gestures towards in his own work on space and place in the *giallo* film when he surmises that the genre exhibits an "ambivalence towards modernity," and that this is "a position affected by the filmmaker (ideally) reflecting these films' vernacular audiences" (46). If we are complicit in this detection of ambivalence, we must accept that it suggests some kind of shift or rupture in the utopian discourse of modernity; this means that, as Dimendberg suggests, such sites of ambivalence might harbor tensions greater than the word "ambivalence" can imply. In his analysis, Koven is very much concerned with the diegetic world of the films—those spaces and places contained within the frame—and their relation to the profilmic physical world. In his view, these films speak, as if by accident, about the spaces in which they are produced. But thinking through Dimendberg's treatment of space in the postwar film noir city can suggest mapping the topography of the *giallo* city in a way that extends the quality of ambivalence into a more sustained critique of modernity. We can trace the same prominence of horizontal organizations of space over the centripetal, with their stable, recognizable centers; in these centrifugal city spaces, the tourist sites of Rome dissolve into an industrialized landscape of office towers, apartment buildings, and empty warehouses. But we also discern a new tonality in the *giallo* world that sets it apart from the centrifugal city of Hollywood film noir; here, narrative action takes place among the *ruins* of modern architecture. In *giallo* cities devoid of recognizable landmarks and historical sites, the promise of expansion, newness, and speed has also fallen away, giving way to dysfunction, abandonment, and decay. The *giallo* is not merely ambivalent about modernity—it confronts us with the ghost town of modernity's utopian dream.

Dimendberg's evocation of centrifugal tendencies in the noir city is also pertinent here because of his description of this space as an *intermediary* moment between the modernist city invoked by Walter Benjamin in his account of Paris in *The Arcades Project* and the city as it is constructed in the postmodern period; these spaces "are historically transitional between an older centripetal metropolis of the street and promenade and the emerging electronic cyberspace of virtual reality and the information superhighway of our present *fin-de-siècle* moment" ("The Will to Motorization" 93). Warped by virtue of its lateness, the modernity of the *giallo* city suggests a significant subset of Dimendberg's intermediary: a moment within a moment that can be distinguished via its particularly dystopian anxiety. One detects it when the resolution of the *giallo*'s narrative cannot overcome the inescapable anonymity and isolation that emanates from its landscape; while Andrea may catch the criminal he pursues through that abandoned industrial landscape, he cannot escape the tonality of this cold, blue-grey world in which the crime narrative plays out. Like those who inhabit Kracauer's hotel lobby, Andrea floats in a void. With no true sense of resolution nor idea of what might come next, the *giallo*'s characters experience time as an endless loop, the way a deep scratch in the shiny black surface of a vinyl record perpetually propels the stylus to replay and play moments from the past.

Dismembering Centrifugal Modernity: Space and Film Style

If we understand Dimendberg's notion of centrifugal space and the postwar film noir to have something in common with these popular Italian films, Wood's interpretation of the *giallo* as the "Italian film noir" extends this relation into a sustained argument for seeing the Italian genre as a direct consequence of the Hollywood noir moment ("Italian Film Noir"). As the previous chapter discusses, this approach forges interesting connections between the two cinemas that further highlight the transnational qualities of the *giallo* film, but this is a relation to be made with caution, lest the Italian genre be subsumed into the murky waters at the margins of the ever-expanding film noir canon. In the first instance, this easy relation can work to obscure the *giallo*'s particular use of film style. While the image of the city in the *giallo* may, at times, recall the centrifugal spaces of the postwar film noir, the camera's treatment of this space produces an image of modernity that belongs to the late-modern moment specifically. City space in the *giallo* world can seem to spiral outward from a misplaced center like the centrifugal spaces in film noirs Dimendberg describes, but this dystopian potential is doubled through the *giallo*'s predilection for abrupt shifts and disruptions to continuity that work against and dismember the sense of spatial wholeness.

So aware is the *giallo* film of the potential for film style to rupture and fragment cinematic space that it plays with this relation continuously. This high level of self-awareness is at play in the scene of the first crime in *The Black Belly of the Tarantula*, where a police inspector dictates the dimensions of the room in which the victim's body has been found. The inspector narrates into a recording device: "The room is rectangular, twelve by eighteen . . . the ceiling nine feet high. It is lighted by a glass wall window, divided into three sections. It's placed centrally, front wall, just above the garden. Period." The rehearsed rhythm and tone of his dictation is punctuated by the flash of the photographer's camera as it captures the body in close-up, then closer again. The inspector's nonchalant manner provides an unsettling contrast to the victim's translucent lemon chiffon nightgown and the garish wound in her stomach. While this type of scene, in which the cataloguing of clues is used to build a hypothesis and hopefully solve the crime, is typical of the process of detection in crime narratives, in *The Black Belly of the Tarantula*, this detailed narration of the particulars of space are like an empty refrain. While this suggests the mundane nature of working the crime scene, it emphasizes the inconsequentiality of the violent act and, above all, the dominance of film style over narrative logic in the film.

The logic of space in the *giallo* is consistently undermined by this film style that often works harder to confuse and disorientate the viewer than to establish or maintain continuity. We could think, once more, of those fragmented images from *The Case of the Bloody Iris*'s opening sequence in the elevator and how they recall the first moments of a number of other *gialli*, including *The Black Belly of the Tarantula*. This film's very first shot, over which the credits appear, frames a partially obscured figure standing behind a filter of forged glass (a panel in the door), which pulls the figure into fragments and reassembles these in the manner of synthetic cubism, so that the figure itself is only just recognizable as human. It obscures no narrative detail or clue, but another figure—of a woman, skin shimmering with oil, reclining while being massaged at an exclusive health club—which the camera's movement slowly reveals. Declaring its fascination with surfaces, texture, and form in its very first moment, the film returns to experimental approaches to the cinematic image throughout; later, a languid and contemplative shot from inside the club swimming pool casts a kind of aesthetic spell on the outside world, rendering the physical space outside the plastic bubble that surrounds the pool foggy and still. Such stylized treatments ask the viewer to focus, and refocus, on the composition of the image by foregrounding its plasticity.

The act of focusing and refocusing is also dealt with in a more concentrated sense in a later sequence where Torrini visits the police photo lab to have a torn photograph of the victim and her lover enlarged and re-enlarged to probe for possible clues. The sequence clearly recalls the similar process undertaken by photographer Thomas (David Hemmings) five years earlier in Michelangelo Antonioni's *Blow Up* (1966); Torrini does unearth a visual clue buried in the grain of the photograph—the vague image of an airplane, but in the *giallo* film, this is no great moment of either clarity or tension. The foregrounding of the process of magnification and dissection of the image is symptomatic of the amateur detective's drive to get to the center of the mystery and to understand where and how things occurred in particular spaces. But this is a drive that can never be satiated in the depthlessness of the *giallo* formula, where it is the actual oscillation between micro and macro perspectives that commands attention, rather than the images' role in maintaining or building narrative logic.

A more pointed instance of this oscillation between perspectival extremes occurs later in *The Black Belly of the Tarantula* when Torrini visits an entomologist for help with his case. As the scientist explains how a particular type of wasp is able to inject a paralyzing venom into its prey, the tarantula, in order to kill it, the image undertakes a jarring leap in perspective from the figures of the two men standing at a desk to an extreme close-up of a wasp and a spider engaged in a struggle. This change in perspective creates an unexpected juxtaposition that foregrounds the impossibility of it occurring within the already established space of the film. When the shot cuts to an image of the entomologist who is narrating the phenomenon to Torrini, the abstraction of this found footage (not even of a tarantula, but of some other smaller, markedly hairless species of spider) cut into the film becomes particularly commanding. As the entomologist explains that the spider's only enemy is "a so-called wasp with salmon colored wings," the extreme close-ups continue and the film shifts register, adopting a documentary aesthetic reminiscent of high school science-class films. This moment of film-within-the-film is structured in a traditional documentary style by the entomologist's voice-of-god narration, but becomes anthropomorphic when the scientist explains that the phenomenon we are witnessing bears a behavioral resemblance to the particular murders Torrini is investigating. The entomologist's lab continues to reveal itself as a conflicted space through the interplay between sound and image when the location of the two characters changes in an abrupt shot that is undermined by the continuity of dialogue in the soundtrack. The scientist's insistence that the victim was "an acquaintance, not a close friend" of the killer is disrupted by a formal play on the jump-cut that not only frames him with a new angle, but has him standing in a completely different part of the room. As in earlier examples, this unpredictable treatment of space is frequently at odds with the order and clarity of the modernist architecture that the films foreground; the uneasy tone this juxtaposition produces is not simply visual excess, but a demonstration of the disorientating effect of the proliferation of perspectives.

The kinds of surveillance mechanisms Dimendberg associates with centrifugal space in film noirs also work in *gialli* to amplify this sense of instability and displacement. While at home one afternoon, Torrini opens his balcony door to let their feline visitor out for a walk and is caught in a wide shot on his modern apartment's balcony. In this moment, we realize that his is just one apartment among hundreds of identical homes and balconies. He goes back inside to make love to with his wife on their new bed, but our voyeuristic experience of their pleasure is disrupted when the shot pulls back out of the balcony window and we learn that we are not the only ones watching. The mechanism that infiltrates the privacy of their home is indicated by the introduction of a mechanical whirring on the film's soundtrack that implicates us in this simultaneous surveillance and voyeurism.

Argento's *Tenebrae* offers a more aggressive instance of how the *giallo* uses style to break or dismember its diegetic space and to promote a milieu of estrangement. Despite being made ten years after both *The Black Belly of the Tarantula* and *The Fifth Cord*, the same late-modern crisis of space, preserved in the genre's system, surfaces to present only a more extreme example of its nightmarish tonality. In *Tenebrae*, the spectacular murder of Tilde and her girlfriend Marion in their ultra-modern apartment constitutes one of the most experimental and strange manipulations of space found in the genre. Marking the beginning of the set piece, an establishing shot of the apartment building announces the structure's explicitly nonclassical style: it is night, and the headlights of a car momentarily illuminate its brutalist facade. Inside the apartment, the split-level design—already fragmentary and compartmentalized—mimics the external aesthetic design of the building. Minimalist white walls, polished boards, and glass paneling around the stairs decorate spaces half-open, half-hidden. In this instance, it is possible that the space matches the friction in Tilde and Marion's open yet dysfunctional relationship; the split nature of their home allows Marion to entertain other lovers and Tilde to fume over her partner's behavior in relative isolation. The fragmented architecture of the apartment is also what allows the killer to slay Marion before Tilde has time to escape, but the architecture's narrative function is significantly overshadowed by the camera's fetishistic exploration of the dwelling. After Marion's latest lover leaves, she leans over the banister, naked but for a strategically wound bedsheet, to call out to Tilde. Standing at the top of the stairs, she resembles a statue of classical antiquity trapped in the modern museum of their blue-white apartment. The warped fidelity of ghostly wind chimes tinkle through the glass-filled apartment, signaling the presence of the killer. These do not sound like real chimes, but Hilda hears them all the same.

The fetishization of the architectural image in *Tenebrae* then shifts into overdrive with an uninterrupted, two-and-a-half-minute shot that sweeps over and around the couple's home. The nightmare quality of the shot is amplified by Goblin's pulsating electronic soundtrack, which also builds suspense as the set piece moves closer to its violent crescendo. Outside the apartment, the frame travels slowly up a wall of vertically arranged bricks, before being interrupted by a window of horizontal blinds. The camera then moves to the left and forwards, even closer to the structure's surface, in a textural study of a section of larger concrete bricks. The frame glides malevolently over a panel of metal shutters, before discovering the window that frames the postcoital goddess upstairs, still wet from her shower. But this voyeuristic tour of the apartment is not over yet, and the camera moves back out of the window and up onto the roof. The micro perspective begins to wreak havoc on the construction of logic and space, becoming even more confusing when the roof tiles become its object of fascination. The cinematography refuses to explain how we, as the killer, are able to realize this experience of space or how we have arrived at another window that frames only that recurrent motif of the *giallo* genre: the apartment staircase. Moving on, the next window offers glossy parquetry floors as a textural contrast to the rough cement brick of the apartment's exterior, before we glide fairly towards a window fortified with heavy horizontal blinds. Although it is not used regularly in *giallo* films, the lumar crane shot here foregrounds the ubiquitous impossibility of escape from the *giallo* world. If this experience of such a fragmented, unpredictable space is possible—if we, as the killer, are able to glide in and around the building like some ungraspable ghost—there's no possibility of closure here.

The apartment is finally infiltrated when the killer uses a heavy pair of metal cutters to snip the links between the blinds, but the film offers no explanation for how this might be possible. Just as we are trying to make sense of where the intruder might be positioned in order to do this, the soundtrack comes to the forefront to rupture the diegesis when Tilde calls to Marion to turn her stereo down. Tilde then hears a disembodied whisper and looks straight into the camera, at us, but there is nobody, but us, there. So, like the victim she always already was, Tilde begins to undress just as the black-gloved hands of the killer appear before us, as if they were our own. A razor slashes a hole in the front of the T-shirt that covers her face, so we can watch her as she dies. Marion's first glimpse of her girlfriend's corpse lying prostrate on the floor in its pool of fresh blood is caught in the doubled and fractured reflection of the scene in the glass-paneled stairs, so that the narrative is propelled forward while the

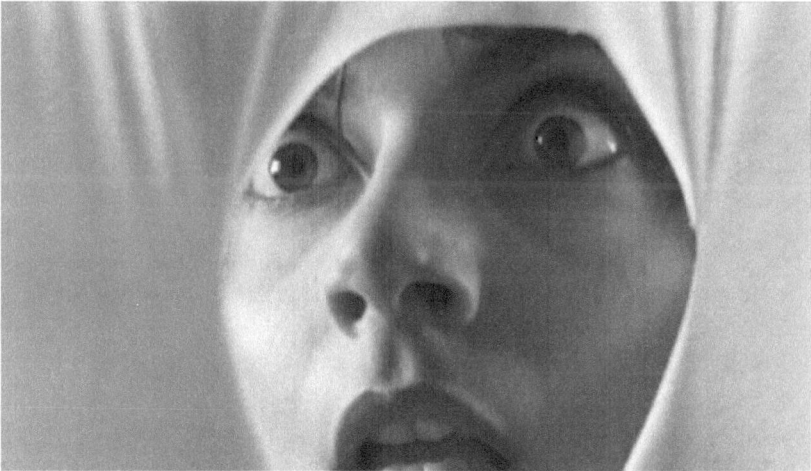

Figure 3.2. Tilde (Mirella D'Angelo) catches a glimpse of her murderer in *Tenebrae* (Dario Argento, 1982). Digital frame enlargement.

distanced, aesthetic experience of the set piece is maintained. As Marion's throat is then slit by the killer, she falls backwards into the same glass panels in which she has just seen her fate, with the film using the full aesthetic potential of the apartment's glassy interior detail.

Argento's inspired use of the lumar crane in this scene constructs a point of view positively unnerving in both its malevolent intent and its impossibility. That the audience identifies in these shots with the killer is a logical and likely conclusion, but the camera's magnified examination of the structure's surfaces and its phantasmagoric movement pulls the viewer's attention away from the construction of linear narrative into a realm of a dark dreamlike logic, where they are forced to observe the architectural detail of a modern home that cannot keep its occupants safe. This is just one example of the identifiable formal patterns the *giallo* film uses to heighten the dystopian potential of its architectural image. In the late-modern *giallo* city, the functionality of architecture born of the International Style's modern aesthetic is not only subverted through formal experimentation but through a treatment of the city and space more broadly that is violent in and of itself. *Giallo* film style takes these already tired, run-down spaces and stretches them with new intensity. It ignores their predetermined purposes or cuts them into pieces, leaving them dismembered and violated like the bodies of this world's inhabitants. In its most urgent moments, as in *Tenebrae*, the functionalist, utopian dream of the modern *giallo* city disintegrates when its architecture becomes an agent of its aestheticized violence. The *giallo* city, like its inhabitants, is always on the brink of collapsing in on itself, perpetually building tension but providing no real relief.

Trapped within a Spider's Web: Horrific Phantasmagorias of the *Intérieur*

> In the recesses of the *intérieur* the bourgeoisie could, for a while, create the illusion of their heroism by surrounding themselves with the costumes of greatness.
>
> —David Frisby, *Fragments of Modernity*

With his story and investigation going nowhere, Andrea decides to visit the home of his ex-partner, Helene (Silvia Monti). She and their young son live in an impressive example of late 1960s Italian architecture: an open plan, design-heavy refuge from the outside world that looks like a showroom of period interior design. What is most interesting about this space in *The Fifth Cord*, however, is how the camera's obsessive fascination with its architectural interior performs a double function, parading the aesthetic while making it difficult to comprehend. Open spaces are blocked with asymmetrical staircases or with bookcases, and an enormous black circular fireplace is suspended from the roof, providing a point of obstruction that the film uses in numerous ways. The bodies of the two characters are arranged in this space in deliberate figurations that, together with the stylized, discontinuous editing, build a mysterious interior that for a short time, relieves Andrea of the mystery that continues to stir, unhinged, outside.

A moment after Andrea lets himself into the house's living room, Helene appears, her figure striking against the mixed canvas of exposed brick and polished wood that make up the walls. But exactly where she stands in relation to Andrea is unclear until an aerial shot of the room transforms the frame into a map of the space and the position of the bodies within it. This momentary establishment of spatial logic is disrupted again, however, when we next adopt Andrea's point of view as he lies on the floor looking up at Helene; relaxing into the retreat that Helene's living room offers, he is shot in close-up from behind the fireplace and as its heat ribbons its way to the top of the frame, Andrea's head ripples like a mirage, oscillating between an image of his face that is whole and one on the verge of disintegrating.

Lounging beside the fire here in the home of his ex-wife, Andrea is enveloped in the space of the private citizen, a contemporary renovation of those spaces that Benjamin called "the phantasmagorias of the interior" of the late twentieth century (quoted in Frisby, *Fragments* 285). This space, into which the citizen retreats from the possibility of transformation envisioned by Marx, was the sanctuary of the everyday—the home and all of its accoutrements: living room sofas, wallpaper, kitchen utensils, bathtubs, and mirrors. Although long days at the office might have us yearn for the respite of home, where we can pad down halls without shoes or defy the summer's heat by showering and remaining undressed, Benjamin's *intérieur* does not grant us respite from the dream we live outside its walls. Rather, it encases us in its own set of mysteries and distractions from the possibility of awakening; as Frisby, quoting Benjamin, writes, "'The *intérieur* of this period is itself a stimulus to intoxication and the dream.' To live within it was to be trapped 'within a spider's web, that dispersed the events of the world, hung up like the dried out bodies of insects'" (247). For Andrea, the significance of this interior potentially offers a doubled encasing from the impending crisis of the outside world; this *intérieur* is both a haven and a portal that enables him to return temporarily to his happier past, a space that helps to construct the memories of a life to which he longs to return. The illusion of this fortification is built from details of the architectural image upon which the camera lingers lovingly: polished wood, abundant neatly arranged bookshelves, a framed photograph, exposed brick walls, the gas-fueled fire and the house's spilt levels. These details are bound by the film to construct a place that seems, at first glance, to provide the characters with the safety associated with the notion of a home. But the camera's phantasmagoric perspectives of the space hint at the devastating possibility that this dream may unravel before our very eyes. When the killer eventually finds his way to Helene's home later in the film, the layers of this interior and its plurality of styles reveal dark, unfinished and cave-like spaces at the center of lower levels of the home. What kind of encasing from the outside world is this?

As Benjamin describes them, the phantasmagorias of the *intérieur* at the turn of the century were conjured through the particular taste culture of the bourgeois that was often characterized by what Frisby calls "a procession of styles" (282). Through film form, the late-modern *giallo* world twists and mutates this procession of styles that, in Benjamin's work on modernity, provides the layers of distraction that attempt to prevent the private citizen from awakening. The uneasy tone that emanates from these spaces is the hum of these restless layers and distractions, as they morph the dream into something closer to a nightmare. The horrific phantasmagoria of the *giallo* interior glimpsed in Helene's home in *The Fifth Cord*—particularly in the hidden, catacomb-like recesses that the house itself encases—realizes its fuller potential in the interior of killer Christiano Berti's ultramodern home in *Tenebrae*. Berti's luxurious late-1970s home encapsulates an unusual juxtaposition between public and private space that is emblematic of Argento's vision of Rome's future. As always, the possibility of such a place existing in the *giallo* world is intercepted by the crime narrative and, even more significantly, by the film text's construction of space.

The credibility of Berti's home as a safe place is in jeopardy from the moment we enter it: the luxury of a well-lit outdoor swimming pool and manicured garden is immediately contrasted with a bare and stripped-back room with an exposed lightbulb hanging from the roof. Two hands in black gloves caress a bunch of neatly filed photographs of the killer's planned next victim. When teenager Maria (Lara Wendel) finds herself stranded on a nearby suburban city street, she becomes the perfect candidate to experience the horrific potential of this home's interior. The serendipity at work in this dystopia means that the teenager, trying to outrun an angry dog, finds herself in the very same stripped-back room we have just visited with the gloved killer. More detail of this cavernous space is revealed as, realizing the gravity of what she is seeing, Maria stuffs the suspicious-looking photographs she finds into her skirt pockets. She circles the edges of the oddly shaped and mazelike room looking for another way out and notices a strip of light under another door. But in a further confusion of classical space, going towards the light in *Tenebrae* is not the path to escape. When Maria enters the main section of Berti's home, looking for help or a telephone, she finds herself completely immersed in this horrific phantasmagoria of the *intérieur*. Like the shot of Andrea and Helene in *The Fifth Cord*, the enormous and luxurious living space is shot from above, like a map of a maze or labyrinth whose floor space is fragmented by designer sofas and raised marble garden beds filled with indoor tropical plants. Searching for a way out, Maria looks as though she is trapped in a glass case. The shot changes to a lower angle, framing her before an array of modern art on the wall hung in salon style, while she tries to call the police. The killer appears opposite her in a wide shot that plays up the contrast between black floors and cold white furniture, punctuated with the glimmer and polish of reflective glass.

Argento's films are particularly potent case studies for investigating these horrific phantasmagorias of *giallo* interiors, as his camera's movement is typically characterized by an eerie fluidity that recalls the dream state. But his intense stylization only brings to the forefront the tension in spatial interiors discernable in most *gialli*. These homes in *giallo* films offer the illusion of an encasing from the impending crisis of modernity going on outside. Filled with the accoutrements of the bourgeois, playing out as a procession of styles that weave a labyrinthine web of distraction, the layers of these interiors build nightmares for their occupants. Watching the *giallo* film, we are pulled into elaborate interiors, which, despite their glassy brilliance, do little to protect us from the void of modern life.

No Place like Home: Ambivalence as Tension

> The presentation of the surface strikes them as an attraction; the tinge of exoticism gives them a pleasurable shudder.
>
> —Siegfried Kracauer, "The Hotel Lobby"

Giallo films harbor a deep fascination with the architectural images of public space, of places of work, and places of inhabitance, but what is particularly striking about the instability fashioned in the *giallo* city is the lack of a sense of home. There is not an absence of homes per se, in the films; as in the examples above, people live in apartments and houses in *giallo* films. However, as the discussion of the interior of Helene's home in *The Fifth Cord* suggests, there is no sense of order or safety in the family or individual's house in this late-modern world. In *Tenebrae*, with the exception of the killer Berti, the characters do not even have homes: protagonist Peter Neale and his assistant Anne spend the entire film traveling and living in hotel rooms. His ex-wife Jane and the killer's shoplifting first victim each live in apartments empty of any signs of life or of the past. In effect, the only past evoked in *Tenebrae* is the dreamlike flashbacks of the primal trauma experienced by the killer, which fuel his violence. As one of the few references to the past in the film, these flashback sequences are distinctly traumatic. They reveal how, as a young man, the killer suffers rejection and humiliation at the hand of an androgynous suitor, who, before an audience of his peers, steps on his head and penetrates his mouth with the heel of her bright red shoes. In a perverse twist on the iconic motif of Dorothy's ruby slippers in *The Wizard of Oz* (1939), this image reinforces the fact that in the *giallo* world there is literally no place like home, in the present or the past.

In *The Black Belly of the Tarantula*, this problem receives a deeper treatment through the characterization of Torrini's wife Anna, who spends almost all the plot time of the film furnishing their home. The presence of stars Giannini and Stefania Sandrelli in *The Black Belly of the Tarantula* means that the home life of the Torrini couple is given substantially more narrative time than a *giallo* might usually allow, but this uncharacteristic narrative weighting also encourages a deeper meditation on the place of home in the film. An interior designer of sorts, Sandrelli's character spends most of the film "homemaking"; she sells old furniture to buy new furniture, sews upholstery, cooks roast chicken dinners, and makes coffee for, and love to, her police detective husband. There is some suggestion that her skills as a homemaker leave something to be desired ("Eggs again?" Torrini asks), but her attempts to conform to and excel in the roles of wife and homemaker preoccupy Sandrelli's character Anna throughout the film. While the genuinely tender and loving relationship in this *giallo* is somewhat unconventional, it is ultimately unable to withstand the disorder of the *giallo* city and the couple are thwarted time and time again in their attempts to live a healthy and happy existence. The hopelessness of these attempts to establish a home life rooted in nostalgia for the past render Anna's desires in this context adolescent, recalling other such couples from cinematic history. Through her refurbishing the couch and cooking dinner, the apartment becomes much like the treehouse Kit (Martin Sheen) and Holly (Sissy Spacek) build in Terrence Malick's *Badlands* (1973). In both cases, these attempts to settle down, furnish a home, and make a life, we know for certain will never succeed. As Anna relaxes into the comfortable bed for which she has traded all of their furniture, and as Holly stares up at the trees, their sadness transforms in its profundity because there is no place, and there will be no place, like the home they are attempting to build.

Although the formula-bound *giallo* film has its roots in ostensibly disposable cheap paperback crime novels that Koven describes as "vacation novels" (47), the working through of the crime narrative ultimately has little bearing on the overall tone of these films. At the conclusion of *The Black Belly of the Tarantula*, the case is solved and Torrini's wife is in a stable condition after her confrontation with the killer. The detective leaves the hospital and steps out into the city street. Walking slowly away from the camera, Torrini is swallowed by the crowds of people who pass through this space as individuals without connection. As he becomes subsumed by the hustle and bustle of the city, he becomes completely anonymous, and a superimposed spider's web begins to weave its way out across the frame, splintering the ordinary city street and the crowd into even further disconnected fragments. This moment is paradigmatic of the cinematic *giallo*'s final moments, which are regularly dominated by a sense of loss. Beneath the murder mystery narrative and the industrially conceived formula that fashions these popular crime films, lays an eerie quality of repetition and emptiness.

4

Those Who Wait

Tourists, Detectives, and Urban Experience in the *Giallo* City

IN THE FIRST YEARS OF THE twentieth century—sometime around 1908—Miss Lucy Honeychurch walks through Florence's Piazza della Signoria, clutching her Baedeker, and she reflects that nothing ever seems to happen to her: "'The world,' she [thinks], 'is certainly full of beautiful things, if only I could come across them'" (Forster 39). This feeling of malaise that arises in moments when, as a young adult, one searches hopelessly for that door into the world where things—experience, passion, love, sex—actually happen, is a universally recognizable encounter. Overcoming it often involves waiting. Nearly a century after Miss Honeychurch's melancholy impatience is described in E. M. Forster's *A Room with a View*—sometime around 1996—nineteen-year-old Lucy Harmon (Liv Tyler), after the death of her mother, travels to Tuscany to stay with family friends for the summer in their villa. In the bath one quiet afternoon, on a torn scrap of paper she writes, "I wait, I wait so patiently. I'm as quiet as a cup. I hope you'll come rattle me. Quick! Come wake me up." In a synchronicity that is no accident, these young women who wait for life to begin to happen to them both travel to Italy, where the promise of adventure founded on the experience of the foreign as exotic is finally satisfied.

This moment of longing and waiting rendered in Forster's 1908 novel, in Bernardo Bertolucci's *Stealing Beauty* (1996), and in myriad other stories—both cinematic and literary—about traveling to Italy is the moment in which the first *giallo* begins: Mario Bava's 1963 film *The Girl Who Knew Too Much* opens with stock footage of a TWA flight heading for Rome. Inside, American teenager Nora Davis (Leticia Roman) sits absorbed in a pulp mystery novel called *The Knife*. She has promised her mother that it will be her last and that she will use her vacation to tame her incorrigible appetite for the five-penny pleasures. What this young crime-fiction fan craves is the sense of adventure that, until now, she has found only on the pages between the yellow covers of these paperback books. But her experience of Italy, framed by both her position as tourist and her penchant for these tales of crime and detection, changes this. Nora's temporary departure from her home and from her day-to-day existence in America facilitates an experience of mystery and adventure in which she plays a central role as the well-read amateur detective. The possibility of this experience depends fundamentally on her traveling to Rome: a city where tourists flock to wander around relics of the classical past, to eat Italian cuisine at old restaurants with silver service, and to frolic on the sand by the sea. This new/old place, which lifts her up and out of her day-to-day existence, transforms Nora both into a tourist on holiday and into an amateur detective who finds herself embroiled in the case of the Alphabet Killer. But sitting on the airplane, buried

Figure 4.1. Roman local Marcello (John Saxon) shows American tourist Nora (Letícia Román) the beauty of the eternal city in Mario Bava's *The Girl Who Knew Too Much* (1963). Digital frame enlargement.

in her murder mystery paperback, Nora does not know this yet. As the opening credits draw to a close, the film's omniscient narrator announces that "this is the story of a vacation."

Certainly, Nora visits the Colosseum and the Piazza Navona. She even meets and begins a relationship with Marcello (John Saxon), a handsome young doctor. But her experience of Italy does not provide the kind of deeply satisfying, life-changing immersion that we have come to expect from this trope. Rather, her journey generates a distinctly ambiguous experience of space and place—and, in particular, the late-modern metropolis—that is subsequently scooped up into the mechanics of the genre and reproduced time and time again in the *giallo* film, to form one of its most paradigmatic concerns. Where the denouement of Lucy Honeychurch's and Lucy Harmon's journeys to Italy both fulfil the romantic potential we are conditioned to expect from the exoticized locale, Nora's time in Italy is also shaped by an experience of the metropolis rooted in the detective novels from which the *giallo* film genre emerges, where the urban environment works to destabilize identity and derail the possibility of personal fulfilment. This oscillation between the types of urban experience offered to Nora begins as soon as the film does, when the narrator's aforementioned claim is, for a moment, juxtaposed with the spy-themed horns of Adriano Celentano's song "Furore." Layered over the opening credits and the stock footage of the TWA airplane as it moves through the clouds, the song gestures towards the highly stylized mysteries that will follow.

This chapter follows Nora, as well as Sam Dalmas, Argento's amateur detective in *The Bird with the Crystal Plumage* (1971), through these shifting identifications to consider how these characters participate as avatars of urban experience in the *giallo* city. Although he lacks Nora's wide-eyed innocence, Sam's expectation of Italy as a source of artistic inspiration and adventure is nevertheless revealed early in Argento's film when, strolling with a friend on the eve of his planned departure, he quips that "everyone said to come to Italy. Nothing has happened to me while I've been in Italy." However, just as soon as he abandons that culturally ingrained hope of Italy's epiphanic effect, Sam's wandering leads him to that place where his position as a tourist in Rome reorganizes into something infinitely more complex: the scene of the crime. As the leisurely strolls of the *giallo* genre's amateur detectives are interrupted by the spectacle of violent scenarios ever more horrific, the films' protagonists move further and further away from achieving the senses of personal growth and resolution that travel narratives have traditionally led us to expect.

Considering the *giallo* genre's cryptic relation to its literary roots and its penchant for disregarding narrative logic, it may seem reasonable to assume that theoretical material developed around historical works of detection is of limited use in coaxing meaning from these seemingly obtuse films. In fact, the opposite is true. Both Benjamin's and Kracauer's interest in the detective novel's relation to the conditions of modernity focuses on urban experiences available in the modern city that can be mapped onto the model of the late-modern *giallo* metropolis with startling resonances. Koven writes that "the *giallo* is a cinema of ambivalence, specifically, ambivalence towards modernity" (58), but interrogating the genre through the prism of this theoretical material reveals how the cinematic genre is principally concerned with the ambivalence that lies at the very heart of modernity itself.

The previous chapter was concerned with the articulation of this sense of unease in space and architecture; here, I seek to uncover this tension in the *giallo* protagonist's *experience* of space. The patterns produced by the vacillating scopic regimes this figure confronts in the late-modern city can be traced along the lines of several types delineated by theorists of modernity, including those of the *flâneur*, the *baudad*, and the *detective*. The types are explored here as three distinct, yet interconnected, encounters with the modern metropolis, with which the *giallo* plays to show how, in the late-modern moment, each of these experiences of the city is on offer to the amateur detective.

Strolling the Streets:
Tourists and *Flâneurs* in the Late-Modern City

> In times of terror, when everybody is something of a conspirator, everybody will be in a situation where he has to play detective. Strolling gives him the best prospects of doing so.
>
> —Walter Benjamin, *The Paris of the Second Empire in Baudelaire*

As the captain announces the airplane's descent into Rome, the gentleman stranger seated beside Nora asks if she would like a cigarette. When he generously extends his offer to include the entire pack, the American teenager accepts with a shy smile and the irrepressible anticipation of adventure, mystery, and romance flickers from behind her cautious demeanor. The teenager is on vacation: a break from her everyday existence that will facilitate a particular way of looking at and being in the space and place of Rome that recalls the scopic regime John Urry has called the "tourist gaze." Urry's theory suggests that, like tourists Lucy

Honeychurch and Lucy Harmon, Nora's trip to Rome will be defined in relation to the place's difference from her quotidian existence in America; her time in Rome will "involve the notion of 'departure,' of a limited breaking with established routines and practices of everyday life and allowing one's senses to engage with a set of stimuli that contract with the everyday and the mundane" (2). As with so many of these stories about young women traveling to Italy, this departure from her everyday existence will also manifest in a romantic encounter, providing a narrative device ideally positioned to exploit the exotic potential of traveling abroad. The romantic interest in these stories tends to assume the role of "guide" to both the unfamiliar geography in which the traveler finds herself and to those often-unfamiliar matters of the heart. In *The Girl Who Knew Too Much*, Nora—with the young doctor Marcello as her guide—visits the Foro Italico and the Colosseum and engages fully in the pleasures of the overrepresented city. Meanwhile, Marcello battles relentlessly to win the young American's heart.

But this time spent as a tourist in Rome exists in a complex relation to Nora's role as a detective, and is the point where this *giallo* bifurcates from the broader group of films about foreigners' journeys to Italy. Unbeknownst to the ardent reader of pulp murder mysteries, this escape from her everyday existence is already structured by the system of expectations she and the film's audience have learned from narratives of detection, and when her elderly host, Ethel, dies during the night, Nora flees the house in search of help into an alternative and significantly darker imagining of Rome. On her way to the Piazza di Spagna, she is mugged and knocked unconscious; upon awakening, she is confronted with a new horror when she becomes the single eyewitness to a violent murder. From this point onward, Nora's engagement with and perception of the city of Rome vacillates between those offered by distinct scopic regimes.

At first glance, the *giallo*'s detection narrative seems to provide the structure for an experience of the urban environment with which the tourist gaze alternates, resulting in a two-faced characterization of the city that relies on that ubiquitous and often prosaic binary of day and night. As Torunn Haaland notes, for Nora, "the experience of Rome will oscillate between these two polar positions—between the romantic but limited dream, and the dark city that, far from curing her from her addiction, will give life to her world of fiction . . ." (139). This doubled experience of Rome is reflected in the film's persistent juxtapositioning of the heavily photographed, overrepresented sites of Rome and examples of relatively anonymous modernist architecture, such as the empty apartment Nora is lured to in her quest to solve the mystery.

Figure 4.2. Nora (Letícia Román) tries to reconcile Rome's contradictory identities in *The Girl Who Knew Too Much* (Mario Bava, 1963). Digital frame enlargement.

The Scalinata di Trinità dei Monti (Spanish Steps) in particular are the location for a number of key moments in this film and Bava uses this well-known tourist site in several interesting ways to convey this perpetually shifting experience of the city. Standing at the door of Laura Craven-Torrani's (Valentina Cortese) apartment, located halfway up the steps, the young American experiences the irreconcilability of these representations of space the film plays with. As the women ascend the few stairs to the door of the apartment, the quintessential tourist site is revealed through glorious, sweeping pans that frame the steps as a series of picture postcards. But when Nora looks back over her shoulder while Laura unlocks the door, she confronts the disjunction between this imagining of the city and the one she experienced on that dreadful night only a couple of days earlier. When Nora tries to reconcile the two experiences of this place by pointing out the spot where the murder occurred, Laura simply declares the event's occurrence impossible.

The film treats Nora's experience of Rome—one constantly shifting between irreconcilable scopic regimes—in a highly reflexive manner. On her return from the hospital, where the doctors reduce Nora's witnessing of the crime to an alcohol-fuelled hallucination, Marcello takes Nora out for the day to see the "real Rome," which he describes as a place 'where the sun shines bright and the air is clear." "A dream perhaps," he declares. "A nightmare, never." As the couple stand on the Scalinata di Trinità dei Monti, now bustling with tourists and Romans in the bright light of day, Marcello invites Nora to consider the beauty of the city: "Just look around you. Does this look like the kind of place women get murdered?" When the young American persists, leading Marcello by the hand to the spot from which she witnessed the murder the previous night, the camera disrupts her staging of the site as a locale for violence when it pans left to reveal a row of fashion models clad in 1960s couture, posing nonchalantly for a photographer. No matter how Nora tries to convince those around her that she did in fact witness a violent crime, the glorious sunshine, glamour, and iconic beauty of the overrepresented city blind those around her to the dark and insidious face of the city that emerges at night. When darkness does fall later that day, mysterious figures emerge from the shadows outside the apartment in which Nora is staying, and she answers her ringing telephone to find no one on the other end of the line. On the arrival of morning, however, the city has returned, again, to the image of its glorious past.

Urry explains how the tourist gaze is defined in part by its focus on specific features of the cityscape that contrast with the tourist's everyday life, but also by the patterns of viewing typical of this engagement that rely on "a much greater sensitivity to visual elements of landscape or townscape than is normally found in everyday life" (3). This protraction of the gaze tends to result in an objectification of specific sites, prompting the impulse to "capture" the moment via the taking of photographs or the purchasing of postcards and souvenirs, which, Urry notes, "enable[s] the gaze to be endlessly reproduced and recaptured" (3). Despite her persistence in discovering the truth behind what she saw the previous evening on the Steps, by day Nora participates fully in this experience of Rome as a collection of particular sites and sights over which to linger. This scopic regime is explored at length in a one-minute montage of Nora and her guide Marcello touring the must-visit sights of Rome, which gives the effect of flicking through the young couple's album of happy holiday snaps. Marcello takes Nora to the Colosseum and to Via Veneto and carries her belongings while she rides, laughing, in a donkey-drawn cart. Spending the day as a tourist certainly goes some way to dispelling the trauma of witnessing the city's darker side, but Nora is never able to settle into a single mode of experience in Rome and the mystery of the crime she has witnessed lures her back into the darkness again and again.

Over time, these two images of Rome become increasingly confused for Nora. As she relaxes by the seaside one afternoon, she is caught unawares by Marcello and for a moment begins to suspect even him of being the murderer. At other times, the complex spilt between these two experiences of Rome is expressed through visual juxtaposition, as in the night when Nora sneaks out alone after receiving a mysterious telephone call. She catches a cab that winds its way through the recognizable cobbled streets of the city before the car pulls up at an old and ornate apartment building. However, when she arrives at the apartment she has been told to visit, she finds an abandoned and anonymous anyplace, where the sense of emptiness is compounded by the sound of howling winds creeping in from outside and the loud click-clacking of Nora's heels on the bare concrete floor. As she stares down a row of naked light bulbs swinging from the ceiling of an empty hallway, a mysterious voice resonates through the emptiness, beckoning her to the end of the hall. Before long Nora discovers that the horror she edges towards is only another referent to the horror others told her she has imagined: a tape recorder playing a prerecorded message. The object is horrifying in itself: when Marcello attempts to play the message back, the couple is sent into a panic by the shrill cacophony of the film's title track "Furore" played at double speed.

The tension and violence confronted by the *giallo* protagonist-as-tourist would seem to contravene Zygmunt Bauman's description of tourism as a highly mediated experience where "shocks come in a package deal with safety" (29); however, in many ways the detection narrative actually serves to exacerbate the contrast between Nora's everyday life and her time in Rome, simultaneously feeding into the expectations of the protagonist and the narrative expectations of the audience. The journey to Italy thus makes possible an encounter with danger that becomes integral to the exoticism of the tourist experience, which, as Urry suggests, is not best encapsulated as a search for authenticity, but by the "basic binary division between the ordinary/everyday and the extraordinary" (368). In this way, the *giallo*'s narrative formula does not limit the potential of the films; rather, the structure of the detection narrative serves to amplify the exotic potential of the text, especially for the nonindigenous viewer particularly predisposed to foreign-as-exotic armchair tourism.

Of course, the link between violence and the foreign exoticized is not particular to the *giallo* film. For Forster's protagonist too, the opening up of Italy's exotic potential pivots on teenager Lucy's witnessing of a violent stabbing in the city center. But the experiences of the city offered by the *giallo* film are very much enabled by the particular combination of the protagonist's journey to Italy as foreign country and the ways the genre draws on classical narratives of detection. As Carlo Salzani writes of crime and detection narratives more broadly, "Crime-as-adventure . . . provides a fictitious escape route: Poe, Alexandre Dumas, and Eugene Sue transform the city into a place of unnameable dangers, menacing shadows, and evil lurking in every door, that is, an *exciting place*" (96).

This darker face of the city takes longer to surface for Sam Dalmas, protagonist of *The Bird with the Crystal Plumage*; the writer has been in Rome "waiting for something to happen" for nearly six months when he decides to give up and go home. Sam's positioning as a tourist is given less narrative time in Argento's film, but it is—again—precisely this transformation of the city from a cluster of overrepresented tourist attractions into a locale for crime that keeps him from boarding his flight back to America. Where Nora's experience of Rome is constantly shifting between the image of the overrepresented city and the more fragmented dystopia of the modern metropolis, Sam—after becoming an eyewitness to the crime—spends the duration of the film trying to come to terms with this dystopian face of the city. After confronting the violent scenario that beckons him into the role of amateur detective, he is no longer able to return to the role of tourist and is forced to come to terms with an increasingly violent and fragmented imagining of the city.

The *giallo* genre's preoccupation with the foreigner in Italy has not gone unnoticed by critics and scholars. Koven suggests that the correlation between the act of traveling and the pulp fiction typically read by travelers could be extended to suggest that *giallo* films can be seen as the cinematic equivalent of "vacation novels," or lightweight paperback pulp fictions designed to be read once and once only. Such claims highlight the genre's fascination with the concept of travel, but also expose assumptions about the way audiences read and construct systems of value around these films. Specifically, equating the *giallo* film with the vacation novel assumes that once the narrative's mystery is deciphered or solved, the film ceases to hold value for the spectator, who, armed already with the mystery's solution, is denied the pleasure of suspense and uncertainty that only the first viewing can ever offer; this leads us quickly back to that scenario where cinema's potential to elicit pleasure and generate meaning is reduced to the level of narrative only. And, as fans of the genre have often argued, the *giallo* is typically uninterested in the development or maintenance of classical narrative cohesion.

What tracing the *giallo* film back to its literary roots does illuminate is that both forms share some fundamental philosophical concerns about the conditions of modernity. Perhaps unsurprisingly, the relation between travel and narratives of detection has been more productively considered by theorists of the genre's literary incarnation, who have tended to investigate more deeply the experiential qualities of the detective novel—including the phenomenon of waiting. David Frisby notes how "the desire to escape 'the flat everyday in time and space' that is a feature of the desire for travel as an end in itself is complemented by a literature appropriate to that travel," leading him to observe that "the detective novel is 'the *ersatz* for the spheres' that are never reached by travel itself" ("Between the Spheres" 8). This suggests that even in the case of classical detective fiction, prioritizing the solution to the narrative's mystery elides some fundamental preoccupations of the detection story. Frisby explains how

> the experiential category of waiting has a wider significance in the context of reading detective novels. The latter are part of what is on offer in the metropolis under the heading which, with his usual insight, Simmel termed the "fillings in of time and consciousness." As Benjamin points out, reading detective novels is associated with the temporary empty time and space or at least the dislocation of time and space on railway journeys. (7)

With Simmel's and Benjamin's observations about the detective novel's preoccupation with "empty time or space" in mind, it is possible to see the *giallo* film's disregard of classical linear narrative more as a strategic rupture than a mere lack of interest. This empty time or space is explored in *giallo* films through a number of identifiable conventions, including an excessive rumination on the motifs of modern forms of transportation that, through repetition and duration, frequently interrupt the continuity of the films' narratives. Needham notes, for instance, the frequency with which airports, airplanes, and the logos of transatlantic airlines appear in the films ("Introduction"). In other *gialli*, the genre's obsession with motifs of travel moves beyond the image of the airplane to include cars and boats, as in Aldo Lado's *Who Saw Her Die?* (1972), which is set in Venice. Others still, like Argento's 2001 *giallo* entry, *Sleepless*, return to that form of modern transportation that was a staple of classical detective fiction: the train. For Koven, this obsession with the motifs of modern travel is a very literal engagement with the "jet-set lifestyle these films are depicting," forming what he sees as "a simplified, more vernacular commentary on the 'economic miracle' than Fellini's *La Dolce Vita*" (49).

Certainly the nation's postwar period of economic boom enabled the development of infrastructure and the possibility of greater travel, but the genre's stylized use of such motifs points elsewhere, too.

In his article "Cinecities in the Sixties," Anthony Easthope posits that the repetition of these motifs can signify more than one attitude to the conditions of modernity. In relation to the notion of utopian cities, he asks:

> Why do we see so much of jet aircraft (never propeller) landing and taking off, taking off and landing, accompanied always by the little puff of smoke and screech when the tyres first hit the tarmac, the symbolic vehicle of the 1960s as much as the car was for the 1930s? Working in excess of what is needed to explain narrative, these repeated airport sequences serve to glorify a utopian vision of intercity technology, a fulfilment of a nineteenth century utopian dream. . . . The optimistic implication is that while some live like that now, in a foreseeable future we will all be able to live like that. (135)

Easthope draws here on the presentation of travel motifs in 1960s films from *The Graduate* (Mike Nicholls, 1967) to the first instalment of the James Bond series *Dr. No* (Terence Young, 1962) as utopian symbols of modernity's potential, but he goes on to talk about dystopian presentations of city space in relation to spaces of anxiety, alienation, and absence drawn from Antonioni's films *L'Avventura* (1960) and *Blow Up* (1966), as well as Jean-Luc Godard's *Alphaville* (1965). The *giallo* film, however, draws from both camps. Utilizing the same iconography of modern transportation as those films with utopian attitudes to the city and modern life, the *giallo* genre's highly stylized formal treatment of these motifs transforms them into agents of rupture, helping to render the modern city as a dystopia. This is evident in the final sequence of *The Bird with the Crystal Plumage*, where the sense of narrative closure we might expect to feel is disrupted by jump cuts to airline branding, shots of the nose of the airplane, and the wheels on the tarmac. This frenetic montage of travel iconography works in excess of the tourism or detection narratives, and the repetition of these formal conventions in *giallo* films shapes a vision of modernity characterized by tension and a loss of certainty.

Considering the extent to which the late-modern *giallo* city is foregrounded as the site of violent spectacle in the films, it is no surprise that Koven, in his writing on the *giallo* as work of detection, moves to consider the genre's protagonist in terms of the quintessential modern social type, the *flâneur*. Theorised in the nineteenth century by Charles Baudelaire as a social type who enjoys a particular engagement with the metropolis characterized by detached observation and a leisurely pace, the concept of the *flâneur* went on to form one of Benjamin's key interests in his work on the city and modernity. For Baudelaire, the *flâneur* was a person who walked the city streets in order to experience the spectacle of modern life; later, Benjamin adopted the concept to describe a way of looking, or a scopic regime, that grew out of the conditions of modernity. This way of experiencing the city that Benjamin describes relies on a particular observer-participant dialectic in which the *flâneur* strolls to observe the spectacle of modern life while maintaining his detachment—and thus individuality—from the activity of the crowd. It is both this dialectic of detached spectatorship and the type's historical periodization that links the *flâneur* to the development of the tourist as a modern social type.

However, because the *giallo* protagonist's experience of the city does not neatly harmonize with any one model of the tourist's, *flâneur*'s, or detective's ways of seeing, Koven surmises that "the amateur detective signifies a strong ambivalence toward the modernity of the *flâneur*" (92). Emphasizing the notion that observation was, for the *flâneur*, an activity of leisure, Koven finds an uneasy lineage between this nineteenth century urban type and the amateur detective of the *giallo*'s late-modern world, also taking issue with the easy relation often made between the *flâneur* and the detective. Although both types are typically found wandering the city streets, "looking for meaning within an inchoate modernity," the chief difference between the two, according to Koven, is that the detective is paid to follow clues and to complete puzzles, whereas the *flâneur* wanders without fiscal concerns or prospects. This leads him to deduce that "those amateur detectives who either do not (need to) work or whose *flânerie* is outside of their paid employment can more accurately be considered a *flâneur*" (94).

Although the *flâneur* model, as both social type and scopic regime, offers significant potential for investigation of the *giallo* amateur detective's experience of the late-modern city, its usefulness for Koven is hampered by an attempt to pin down the complex classificatory history of the term. As Haaland observes, defining the detective in relation to the matter of payment, for instance, is problematized by the fact that

> detection . . . is rarely only or even mainly about payment for a mission. One single common feature that may be said to relate such different figures as Sherlock Holmes, Sam Spade, James Bond and George Smiley, is precisely the lack of consideration for what may be modest pay and scarce, if any, credit for cases they have completed with other than material motivations. (130–31)

Haaland is not the first to observe that the detective's profession is almost always more than a way to pay the rent. As Franco Moretti writes of Sherlock Holmes, the detective "lives to serve this impersonal thing, detection. He does not use it for personal gain: 'As to reward, my profession is its own reward' ('The Adventure of the Speckled Band')" (244). It is the detective's obsessive interrogative gaze that leads Moretti to describe his dedication to the art of detection as "dilettantism":

> Dilettantism is not superficiality, but work for the pleasure of work: "To the man who loves art for its own sake . . . it is frequently in its least important and lowliest manifestations that the keenest pleasure is to be derived" ("The Adventure of the Copper Beeches"). Thus, Holmes is not a policeman, but a decadent intellectual. (245–46)

Although the term "dilettante" has come to be used disparagingly to imply someone is an "amateur," Moretti's description refers to earlier uses of the term that described a person who does not work as a professional artist, but nevertheless engages passionately with and promotes the fine arts. To describe the detective as dilettante then, emphasizes the detective's covetous passion for the process of detection and suggests that, as Haaland observes, narratives of detection are little concerned with the profession as a means of paid employment. The notion of detective as dilettante, or one who loves to scrutinize the city, recalls the relationship between the detective, the *flâneur*, and the tourist as social types, for it is this very enthusiasm for reading the detail of the modern metropolis as text that forms one of the *flâneur*'s most significant activities, too. These relations also begin to demonstrate the impossibility of developing clear-cut models of urban "types" with which to interrogate the modern city. In fact, thinking through the concept of the *flâneur* and how the figure relates to the late-modern urban experience of the *giallo* film's protagonist can help to illustrate just how unstable Benjamin's characterization of the *flâneur* actually is, by rehearsing the shifting nature of urban experience in the modern city. As Tom Gunning writes, "I think it is worth stressing the way the *flâneur* gave way to other avatars of urban experience, however much they may maintain a strong relation to their original archetype"; the figure of the amateur detective in the *giallo* film can help us to do this (27).

In trying to maintain the distinction between *flânerie* as it has been historically understood and the tourist-turned-detective the *giallo* genre takes up as its protagonist, Haaland refers to amateur detectives as "detective-*flâneur*[s]" who find themselves in an "ambiguous position" (130). He argues that because the darker, late-modern city confronted by these characters typically produces spectacles of violence, their wandering "is too distracted to achieve the errant and personally fulfilling nature of *flânerie*" (130). But critics have tended to romanticize the fulfilling nature of the *flâneur*'s city walks, effectively freezing the avatar as an icon of urban spectatorship that simply persists—or ceases to be—as modernity continues to unfold. As Gunning points out, however, even "for Benjamin the *flâneur* marked a transitional phase of modern urban geography, like the arcades in which he strolled, disappearing as Paris fully entered into modernity" (27). In other words, as the modern city grew and changed, the *flâneur*'s engagement with it developed into new modes of urban experience.

The moment where the gaze refocuses from the scopic regime of the *flâneur* to achieve the scrutiny and interrogation required of detection was imagined by Edgar Allen Poe in his 1840 story "The Man of the Crowd," a piece that Benjamin calls "something like an x-ray of a detective story" (Gunning 27):

> At first my observations took an abstract and generalizing turn. I looked at the passengers in masses, and thought of them in their aggregate relations. Soon, however, I descended to details, and regarded with minute interest the innumerable varieties of figure, dress, air, gait, visage, and expression of countenance. (Poe, "Man" 216)

This moment of "descent into detail," when the scopic regime of detection is born, is precisely the shift that the *giallo* tourist/*flâneur* experiences, provoked by their confrontation with the spectacle of violence in the modern city. But the *giallo* amateur detective's metamorphosis into this new way of seeing does not happen with the ease and clarity of Poe's classical detectives. In fact, it is interrupted by another transitory moment that has more in common with the less-considered figure of the *badaud*. As Gunning explains, "These three ideal types may shade into each other within the course of a narrative (as the narrator of [Poe's] story moves from his reverie of detached *flânerie* to his detective-like shadowing of the old man), but they can also be morphologically distinguished" (2). When the detachment and leisurely pace of the *giallo*'s foreigner-protagonist is disrupted by the aesthetic shock of violent crime in the late-modern city, their ways of seeing begin to vacillate between that of *flânerie* and the multiple optical regimes it historically gave rise to.

From *Flâneur* to *Badaud*:
Moments of Shock in the Late-Modern City

On the eve of his planned departure from Rome, Sam is whistling as he strolls down a quiet Roman city street. The luminosity of a brightly lit gallery across the road pulls his shadow from him and stretches it across a concrete wall mottled with stains from poster glue. This light rouses Sam's contemplative gaze, inviting him to focus his attention; adjusting to this shift in modes of observation, his brow furrows and his pace slows, while he blinks in disbelief. He moves closer to the edge of the road to get a better look, then stops dead in the realization that he is witnessing the murder of a woman take place on the gallery's upper

Figure 4.3. Foreigner Sam Dalmas (Tony Musante) is caught off guard while strolling in Rome in *The Bird with the Crystal Plumage* (Dario Argento, 1970). Digital frame enlargement.

level. A shot of the street from inside the gallery captures the wandering writer's experience of this moment of shock: with his hands still in his pocket from his leisurely stroll, Sam now stands completely still, mouth agape, transfixed by the spectacle of violence unfolding behind the glass façade of the gallery. In this moment, Sam embodies the urban type of the *badaud*.

This moment of shock that manifests so unmistakably in the physical body is interrupted by the suddenly loud horn of a car that clips Sam as he realizes he has stepped onto the road. This second disturbance propels him forward through the disengagement of the *badaud* moment into action and he runs across the street to help the woman who is struggling down the gallery's stairs with the killer's knife planted firmly in her back. But this moment of stasis that punctuates the shift in urban experience and scopic regimes for the *giallo* protagonist is worth considering, because it suggests that—particularly in the late modern period—the shift from the *flâneur*'s way of seeing to the detective's has dimensions that require further complication.

For Gunning, Poe's story "The Man of the Crowd" demonstrates how the *flâneur*'s characteristically cool observation began yielding to "a related but more powerful form of fascination" with the modern metropolis in the early modern period; in the case of Poe's description, this shift is reflected in his narrator's sudden and compulsive interest in a solitary figure he notices within the crowd. The narrator's fresh and intense interest in this one strange "man of the crowd" propels him from his detached mode of observation—in which the crowd is viewed as spectacle—to adopt a scrutinizing gaze, or an optical regime aligned with the gaze of the detective. As Gunning observes, this shift in the narrator's way of seeing (from *flâneur* to detective) is facilitated by his witnessing the hideous spectacle of this gawking and desperate stranger (the *badaud*), thus forming a trichotomy of urban types operating in the modern metropolis. Gunning sees both the *badaud* and the detective as types that bifurcate from the *flâneur* as a result of the increasingly fragmentary and violent nature of the life in the city. In the late-modern world of the *giallo*, however, this relation between ways of seeing is even more complex. When the role of the detective is assumed by an amateur, this zoom in from detached observation to focused scrutiny is almost always mediated by the paralyzing experience of becoming an eyewitness, or a moment in which the protagonist more closely resembles the glaring inertia of the *badaud*.

In most readings of this less-explored type, the *badaud* is figured as a kind of opposite of the detective, and, although Benjamin never explored this avatar of urban experience in great detail, his contrasting of the two figures can help us to understand the qualities of the *badaud*'s observation:

> In the *flâneur*, the joy of watching is triumphant. It can concentrate on observation; the result is the amateur detective. Or it can stagnate in the gaper; then the *flâneur* has turned into the *badaud*. (Gunning 62)

As Gregory Shaya explains, *badaud* was often translated as "gawker," carrying with it the connotations of idle curiosity, gullibility, simple-minded foolishness, and gaping ignorance. *Grande dictionnaire universel* (1867) defined it in this way: "The *badaud* is curious; he is astonished by everything he sees; he believes everything he hears, and he shows his contentment or his surprise by his open, gaping mouth." The images conjured by such descriptions reveal a type of engagement with the city almost diametrically opposed to the others worked through by theorists of modernity. If the *flâneur* is detached from the crowd, the *badaud* is at one with it. If the detective adopts a scientific scrutiny of the dark and violent city to resolve its mysteries, the *badaud* succumbs to curiosity and stares unashamedly at its spectacle (5).

To disrupt the political problematic of this urban type, Shaya looks instead to the depiction of the *badaud* generated by the early twentieth-century Parisian press and discovers traces of this urban experience where "the coming together of people in the street was presented as a sign of empathy and insight and not as a sign of simplemindedness" (6). Most significantly, Shaya uses the images disseminated by the press in this period to argue that the open and gaping mouth of the *badaud* is misrecognized as the "mark of gullible stupefaction," when in fact it often expresses a bodily reaction to horror and the moment of shock (11).

Shaya finds a parallel for this increasingly overwhelming experience of the modern metropolis in Baudelaire's image of the *flâneur*, whom he sees as a type "frequently overstrained by the experience of the city" (48). Where so many readings of the *flâneur* focus on the leisurely pace and detached contentment of the figure, in poems such as Baudelaire's "The Seven Old Men" (1859), Shaya detects traces of the *flâneur*'s increasingly fragmented and dark experience of the modern city, which is not only a kaleidoscopic spectacle of amusement for the *flâneur*, but a horrifying place where the *flâneur* finds himself, in Bejamin's words, "steeling . . . [his] . . . nerves to play a hero's part" ("Paris of the Second Empire"). The fact that the modern city elicits shocks and horrors which affect not only the undereducated masses, but those who intellectualize the experience and spectacle of the city too, foregrounds the instability of those avatars of urban experience developed to theorize ways of looking developed through modernity.

Returning to Poe's story we also find, in a less-often quoted section, a moment when the narrator describes a confrontation that suspends him in time. Sitting in the dark, splendid night, the narrator suddenly comes upon a countenance "which at once arrested and absorbed my whole attention":

> As I endeavored, during the brief minute of my original survey, to form some analysis of the meaning conveyed, there arose confusedly and paradoxically within my mind, the ideas of vast mental power, of caution, of penuriousness, of avarice, of coolness, of malice, of bloodthirstiness, of triumph, of merriment, of excessive terror, of intense—of supreme despair. I felt singularly aroused, startled, fascinated. "How wild a history," I said to myself, "is written within that bosom!" (218)

The excessive terror apparent in the image of this man of the crowd provokes in the narrator—if only for a "brief minute"—the characteristics of the *badaud*. As Poe's narrator struggles to come to terms with the horror before him, his mental picture is expressed in the *badaud*'s physicality.

Figure 4.4. The tourist becomes the eyewitness in *The Girl Who Knew Too Much* (Mario Bava, 1963). Digital frame enlargement.

This figuration of the body—static but for eyelids blinking in disbelief, mouth agape—is rehearsed time and time again by the *giallo* protagonist in the moment they become eyewitnesses to the crime.

This pattern of shifting scopic regimes and its figural expression is also clearly recognizable in Nora's face as she bears witness to the act of violence on the Spanish Steps the night she flees the apartment of her (very) recently deceased host. Clutching her raincoat closed against the storm, she descends the stairs hurriedly and does not see her assailant lurking behind a high wall in the foreground of the shot. As she draws closer, the figure creeps across the frame to intercept the young American and strikes to snatch her bag, pushing her to the cobblestoned street. Nora is out cold, and lays prostrate on the steps while her patent coat glistens in the night, gaping to expose her bare legs.

An indeterminate amount of time passes before Nora awakens, shivering and disheveled, and struggles to pull herself up against a stone banister. Glassy-eyed and confused from the impact of her fall, she tries to steady herself when a clock suddenly strikes twice and a terrifying cry of pain reverberates through the still night. She looks around, but her vision is blurred and hazy. Suddenly through the fogginess ahead, Nora makes out the figure of a woman struggling to stand up. The woman lurches towards her—through the empty night—collapsing to reveal a knife planted firmly in her back. Nora's eyes widen, her mouth is agape, and she is struck by the same paralyzing moment of recognition that Sam faces outside the gallery. Unlike Sam, however, Nora's recovery from this temporary paralysis and shock is complicated by her having hit her head; dizzy from her fall, she cannot instantly shift into action and overcome the *badaud* moment. Instead, fearing for her own safety, she retreats and crouches behind a banister. Nevertheless, she continues to look. Nora watches as a second figure emerges from the shadows to pull the knife from the body and drag it back into the darkness, and she bears witness to the violent scenario, transfixed by fear, until her eyesight begins to blur once more and she collapses back down onto the street. It begins to rain. Unconscious and alone on the steps after this second trauma, Nora is stripped of her agency to act, fixed in the scopic regime of the *badaud*. Bava mirrors the ambiguity of vision that Nora has experienced when he pans to a puddle of water collecting beside her. Disturbed by the rain, the reflection of the overrepresented image of Rome begins to quiver, fragment, and finally dissolve.

When Nora awakens the following day in the hospital, she is troubled both by her foggy recollection of the event and the realization that no one believes her story. It is this doubled misrecognition that propels her to solve the mystery herself. Although Nora's experience as the *badaud* is stretched in terms of duration, both she and Sam are mobilized beyond this paralyzing vision through their need to restore order by deciphering the mysteries of the violent crimes they have borne witness to. But in this moment of the gawker, as Sam and Nora stand, mouths agape, before the spectacle of violence in the modern city, their characters are responding to scenarios of extreme violence as moments of shock. More than stupefaction, the physical manifestations of shock mark the amateur detective's shift from the tourist/*flânuer*'s experience of the city to those increasingly summoned by the dystopian late-modern metropolis.

The figure of the amateur detective in the *giallo* foregrounds the transitory nature of the *badaud*'s experience, which Shaya refers to as a "vision . . . always in need of being completed. The emotional [and physical] response opened the way to lamentations, investigations and calls to action"; in the case of the *giallo*, the protagonists' *badaud* moments are the necessary preamble to their adoption of that scrutinizing gaze that belongs to the detective (Shaya 25). If, as Benjamin predicted, this future is a place where everyone is thrown into playing the role of detective, it is because the stroller experiences the shock of the city's increasingly violent nature and is perpetually troubled by the irreconcilability of the scenarios she bears witness to.

Descending to Details:
From *Badaud* to Amateur Detective

When Shaya writes of the *badaud*'s vision as something that needs to be "completed," he foregrounds the transient qualities of this scopic regime; indeed, the state of temporary stasis and shock experienced by the *giallo* protagonist in the late-modern city motivates the foreigner to adopt yet another new way of seeing (25). The *badaud*'s vision can open out into a range of new experiences of the city, but this experience of shock always propels the *giallo* protagonist towards the scopic regime of that quintessential modern figure, the detective. Where the *badaud*'s experience of the city is characterized by idle passivity, the detective's gaze meets the modern metropolis with a focus on observation and analysis, rather more like the *flâneur*'s. Only now, the outsider must put this systematic way of seeing to work, in order to restore balance to the city made chaotic through the eruption of violence and crime.

For Dana Brand, the necessity of these shifts in scopic regimes is reflected more broadly in each type's particular understanding of the modern metropolis: "The city of Poe's detective stories contains a profusion of interpretive languages as well as profusion of opaque texts. It differs markedly from the *flâneur*'s city in which there is only the *flâneur*'s language and in which every face and object can be easily read" (228). In other words, the *flâneur*'s urban experience is one relatively untroubled by illegible signs. As both Brand and Shaya note, the reading strategies of the *flâneur* certainly develop in response to the growing urban anxiety and dislocation of modernity, but these anxieties are processed and recuperated through the *flâneur*'s detached observation and production of text:

> In the literature of the *flâneur*, the reader is shielded from all potential sources of anxiety at the moment he encounters them. When, for example, the *flâneur* acknowledges the ability of a rapidly changing city to obliterate the traces of the individual, he will do so in the act of recovering the traces. (229)

Like the *flâneur*, the detective is never a man of the crowd, but observes the spectacle of the city from a privileged and distanced position, and as Brand has pointed out, the detective's gaze as panoramic as the *flâneur*'s (237). The detective is distinct, however, in being able to mobilize this vision to master the text of the modern city, to solve the mystery of the crime and restore order. The detective adopts a range of interpretive techniques to navigate and decipher the modern city: a place of shadows and mystery, paved with what T. S. Eliot called "streets . . . of insidious intent" ("Love Song of J. Alfred Prufrock," lines 8–9). To uncover clues in the complex fabric of the city text, the detective draws on refined observational skill and applies logic and rationality to objects of the gaze; the shift from looking to scrutiny is driven by an aim to bring the world destablized by the crime back into alignment. To do this, the detective often relies on the forms of quintessentially modern transportation and communication. As Moretti, in his essay "Clues," points out, trains, telegrams, carriages, and letters form indispensable narrative devices in such stories, where these modern technologies are invariably reliable (246). Amid the chaos of the unsolved crime, the detective's navigation of the increasingly complex metropolis via these modern technologies smacks of the utopian potential of modernity. As Moretti notes, "Society expands and becomes more complicated: but it creates a framework of control, a network of relationships, that hold it more firmly together than ever before" (246–47).

The shift from *flâneur* to detective was necessary in order to mediate and reflect a growing anxiety in the modern metropolis. For the reader of classical detective fiction, the masterful "mole's eye view" of the detective could facilitate "controlled exposure" to this darker and increasingly complex side of modern life (Moretti 37). The narrative structure of the detective novel, developed through the figures of Poe's Dupin and, later, Arthur Conan Doyle's Sherlock Holmes, provided an armchair tourist's guide to the dystopian metropolis, offering the double pleasure of experiencing "both the epistemological and physical anxiety in the city and . . . its resolution" (Brand 229). Moretti explains how the culture developed through Conan Doyle's Sherlock Holmes stories works to resolve

> the deep anxiety of an expanding society: the fear that development might liberate centrifugal space energies and thus make effective social control impossible. This problem emerges fully in the *metropolis*, where anonymity—that is, impunity—potentially reigns and which is rapidly becoming a tangled and inaccessible hiding place. (246)

In this light, the detective's way of seeing provides reassurance. In a period of rapid change and expansion, the figure of the detective demonstrates that, despite its ambiguity, the modern city can be controlled and understood. But theorists of modernity have questioned the extent to which any detection story's narrative resolution provides an adequate sense of closure or a true restoration of order and this is an issue that requires further complication before moving on to consider how the *giallo* genre engages with this classical narrative structure.

The modern detective novel has been analyzed as a unique cultural form by a range of theorists and critics, including Benjamin, Kracauer, and Bertolt Brecht. Todd Herzog even suggests that work by these thinkers on the subject can be thought of discursively as a "German modernist theory of detection fiction," because although each of these writers privileges different aspects of the genre, there are two significant points of convergence in their interest in modern detective fiction (25). Firstly, each theorist agrees that the popular genre of detective fiction is a valuable tool for thinking through the conditions of modernity. Herzog explains how all three "read detective novels as unconsciously avant-garde texts that function as mass-market versions of elite modernist works" that question "the place of the subject in the modern world, the negotiation of urban space, and the dysfunctionality of reason and causality" (25). Conceptualizing a German modernist theory of detective fiction as a discursive approach to the detective novel offers us a reading protocol that behaves significantly like the cult cinema paradigm, where collective championing of the underrepresented or marginalized text has the power to reposition and reinvigorate and to uncover new possibilities of meaning. Reading against the grain of these pulp fictions, modernist theorists' uncover a significantly complex critique of the culture that produces the detective novel, embedded in their text.

Secondly, via this alternative approach, German modernist theory of detective fiction is interested particularly in the reader-text relationship, seeing the role of the reader as active and participatory:

> In these theories, readers turn to detective fiction in search of a narrative that gives form and meaning to their inscrutable lived experience. For Benjamin, detective novels convert the strangeness of the city into mystery, thus rendering it potentially knowable. For Brecht, they resurrect the laws of causality that no longer function in life. For Kracauer, they act as a distorted mirror that reflects a thoroughly rationalized and derealized society. These readers find themselves lost in modernity, and the detective novel responds to their situation and compensates for it. (Herzog 25)

According to Herzog, this understanding of the detective novel's reader contrasts dramatically with the dominant perception of such genres and their audiences. Instead of positioning these popular texts as escapist, German modernists look beneath the auxiliary generic structures to discover that which provides the reader with sophisticated commentary on the conditions of modern life and the paradoxes of modernity (25).

For the purposes of understanding how the *giallo* film relates to these earlier readings of the detective story, we might look to the writing of Kracauer in particular. An avid reader of detective fiction, Kracauer reviewed newly published detective novels in German daily newspaper *Frankfurter Zeitung*. His most extensive theoretical work on the genre, however, is the 1925 book *Der Detektiv-Roman* (*The Detective Novel*), from which "The Hotel Lobby" originates. Although the rest of this work remains untranslated from German, Gertrud Koch cites *Der Detektiv-Roman* as a particularly comprehensive work that "brings together almost all the themes of significance to Kracauer in his early work," where the theorist "sets out to analyze the phenomenon of the detective novel as a 'translation' of human existence" (Koch 16).

More than the actual narrative mysteries of classical detective fiction, it is the characters who populate detective novels that intrigue both Kracauer and Benjamin. Particularly, it is the genre's typical characters that are important: the detective, the criminal, and the police. Never individuals with truly unique characteristics, these are figures who instead represent intellectual concepts or particular relationships to the modern world. Because of this tendency for the detective narrative's characters to function as types, Moretti claims that detective fiction is "radically anti-novelistic":

> The aim of the narration is no longer the character's development into autonomy, or a change from the initial situation, or the presentation of plot as a conflict and an evolutionary spiral, image of a developing world that is difficult to draw to a close. On the contrary: detective fiction's objective is to *return to the beginning*. The individual initiates the narration not because he lives—but because he *dies*. (241)

Like classical detective fiction, the *giallo* film is rarely concerned with character development or evolutionary narrative spirals. In fact, the cinematic genre specifically foregrounds and extends the formula's anti-novelistic qualities to fashion what Moretti describes as "the nightmare of detective fiction": a world where the restoration of order is perpetually thwarted by "the perfect crime . . . the featureless, deindividualized crime that anyone could have committed because at this point everyone is the same" (238). The *giallo* killer is not necessarily the perfect criminal, but as a recurrent character type operating within the late-modern city, the killer's motives are unfathomable to the point of deindividualization (Moretti 238). Where Moretti identifies three criminal types in classical detective fiction—the noble, the upstart, and the stepfather—as Paul Johnson observes, the majority of the *giallo* film's violence is triggered by a latent psychological trauma embedded in the killer's subconscious. In both *The Girl Who Knew Too Much* and *The Bird with the Crystal Plumage*, murder is motivated by past experience of violence or the attempt to conceal trauma this experience has caused. As amateur detectives, both Nora and Sam succeed in unearthing some trace of the killer by adopting the classical detective's strategies of logic and rational deduction, but because the true motivations for violence are concealed within the killer's subconscious, the processes of classical detection are rarely able to lead the *giallo*'s amateur detective to fully solve the crime.

The *giallo*'s amateur detective is, however, much like the classical detective, "not moved by pity for the victim, by moral or material horror at the crime, but by its *cultural quality*: by its *uniqueness* and its *mystery*" (Moretti 239; emphasis in original). For Kracauer, this relation to the other characters who populate the detective story is governed by the role of the detective as a "representative—even a personification—of reason (*ratio*): 'He doesn't focus on reason, he is its personification'" (Herzog 139; quoting Kracauer). This positions the detective in a triangulation of character types in the detection narrative, where personal investment in the case has little to do with helping the police to uphold the law (although the detective may claim this is the case). Neither does the detective identify with the criminal, however, who breaches it. Instead, the detective is consumed by "the process of solving the puzzle that the crime presents" (Herzog 166).

But the intensity of the detective figure's engagement with the crime in the *giallo* is amplified by the particular nature of this entanglement; the *giallo*'s amateur detective is not called to the scene of the crime to be consulted as a specialist, but is drawn into the mystery through their temporary embodiment of the *badaud* type in the moment of witness.

In the manifestation of that world that Benjamin foresaw, where "everybody will be in a situation where he has to play detective" ("Paris of the Second Empire" 21), the amateur detective's drive to solve the crime is bound up with the attempt to reestablish the order of their world (Johnson). Because of the ambiguity inherent in this new triangulation of character types, in which the detective is also eyewitness, the *giallo* protagonist often becomes a suspect, too. It is under this presumption that Sam is detained by Roman police in *The Bird with The Crystal Plumage* and is unable to return to America on the date he had planned.

The *giallo* amateur detective's misrecognition of detail or "truth" during the moment of shock means that their accounts of the violent scenarios are often contextualized as unreliable. In his *Kinoeye* introduction to the genre, Needham shows how the notion of the eyewitness, or *testimone occulare*, is fundamentally important to the *giallo* genre, especially in terms of the way the films use the construct to play with notions of truth and authority. Writing on *The Bird with the Crystal Plumage*, he notes how

> the gallery is explicitly concerned with maximising clarity and vision: the space is minimal so there are no distractions for the gaze other than that of the crime; the doors/façade are enormous glass panels; nothing is obscured; the entire area is brightly lit. However, despite all of these supports aiding Dalmas's vision, he fails to see (or in psychoanalytic terms, he *misrecognises*) the truth of his gaze. ("Introduction"; emphasis in original)

In order to rewrite the misrecognition, Sam returns to the scene of the crime and reenacts the struggle he believes to have taken place. But it is not until much later that he finally realizes he has misread the scene and misrecognized the criminal as the victim.

In *The Girl Who Knew Too Much*, the amateur detective's misrecognition is facilitated by the mugger who knocks Nora unconscious earlier in the evening. When she awakens with fuzzy vision, she witnesses the murder, but is too debilitated by the fall to flee or intervene. For Nora, this positioning as unreliable is compounded by both her age and gender and she is denounced as a delusional alcoholic, then a psychic time-traveler, before she is recognized as an eyewitness by the male authority figures who surround her.

In other *gialli*, this ambiguity is exploited to fashion narrative twists: Argento's 1982 film *Tenebrae* has the amateur detective take over the role of criminal after he becomes eyewitness to the first crime. While Argento flips the possibilities for each character type over and over again in *Tenebrae*, his protagonist, Peter Neal, quotes Conan Doyle's *The Hound of the Baskervilles* while he sorts through the clues he has amassed. Trying to apply those classical principles of logic and rational deduction he learned from the master writers of popular fiction, he recites, "When you have eliminated the impossible, what remains—however improbable—must be the truth." But in this increasingly fragmented world, there is no glory in the discovery of truth. As Johnson writes, "While the classical detective is able to apply his recognized ability to read the crime scene and clues, the amateur detective seems to fumble his way to the unmasking of the transgressor through a process of trial and error. It is more by luck than judgment that the killer's identity is revealed at the closure of the narrative."

The amateur detective's misrecognition, or failure of vision, is a trope that betrays the *giallo* as a late-modern genre, for it can be traced sideways into examples of more widely canonized modern European art cinema such as Antonioni's *Blow Up*. This connection is often made via *Deep Red* (1975), because Argento has acknowledged the influence of Antonioni's film on his own. But the more important connection to be made lies in the films' questioning ways of seeing in late modernity, through the figure of the amateur detective. The *giallo* genre takes the trope foregrounded in *Blow Up*'s well-known sequence of photographer Thomas's (David Hemmings) magnification of his pictures as one of its unifying generic principles, absorbing into its very formula the increasingly fragmented nature of experience in the modern world.

Those Who Wait

Gunning writes that "both the detective and the classical spectator of narrative cinema are trying to make sense of what they see, and both believe that this project is possible" (36). The *giallo*'s amateur detective harbors this same belief, but the films are rarely able to conceal the fact that the world they inhabit is unknowable, impenetrable, and strange. In the most fascinating examples of the genre, this strangeness, which is sometimes expressed as kitsch, is barely containable; it bleeds out over any restoration of order and stunts any sense of closure.

The irreconcilability of the two sides of Rome that Nora experiences in her double role of tourist/detective is maintained throughout *The Girl Who Knew Too Much*, so that the film never settles on a single or knowable image of the eternal city. This already unstable characterization of Rome is, in the final sequence, pushed into the realm of kitsch when Nora discovers the packet of cigarettes the stranger had given her on the airplane in her bag. Only then does she remember that she had smoked one before hearing that they were "marijuana cigarettes" and is suddenly struck by the possibility that the entire crime narrative may have been a drug-induced hallucination. With this realization, she throws the packet of laced cigarettes over a bridge. While she and Marcello wander off into the sunset, a young priest strolling beneath them sees the packet fall from the sky, picks it up and stashes it within his robe.

While Nora may have, in some way, finally made sense of what she saw on her first night in Rome, this saccharine ending ensures that the spectator cannot. And while the often snappy and upbeat tone of Bava's film diffuses the uneasiness produced by this instability, in many of the *giallo* films that follow it, including *The Bird with The Crystal Plumage*, it is the unsettling quality of the kitsch ending that prevails. Although they adopt the scopic regime of the detective, neither Sam nor Nora's *badaud* misrecognition is unraveled in time for them to solve the crime. Instead, they are drawn blindly into, and rescued from, climactic and potentially fatal encounters with the killer. In this way, the *giallo* film foregrounds the impossibility of classical detection's project to "make sense of what one sees"; to experience its modernity is to adopt multiple, shifting scopic regimes in a fragmented, dissolving, and unknowable world. Whether they know it or not, this makes Sam and Nora what Kracauer describes in his essay "Those Who Wait" as "companions in misfortune" (129).

Kracauer says that "the detective explores the surface of everyday life. It is a surface that has no depth; nothing lies beneath it; clues are hidden by other clues, things by other things" (130). In some *giallo* films, the element of kitsch that reveals this is displaced entirely by some irrefutable glimpse of modernity's disconnectedness, of the fissures that disrupt the possibility of a knowable world. In the final shot of *Deep Red*, Marcus Daly stares into an image of himself reflected on the glimmering surface of a pool of blood. As the closing credits run over the shot, Marcus is caught in the intermediate realm between nostalgic desire for the restoration of order and simultaneous recognition of the surface being all there really is. As Frisby notes, "The fact that things merely 'happen' and 'are' without meaning only serves to increase our thirst for knowledge of the totality. This is supplied by the detective novel, which creates an aesthetic self-referential totality of a world of events as things" ("Between the Spheres" 20). But the *giallo* world never offers us this totality, except as some nostalgic impossibility. Caught in Kracauer's intermediary realm, the *giallo*'s protagonists live in a kind of feedback loop, where all there really is to do, is wait.

In the final sequence of *The Bird with the Crystal Plumage*, Sam and his partner Julia wait to return to America and, ostensibly, to their everyday lives. The kitsch of this ending is almost Sirkian in the way the film's form plays against and muddles the happy ending cliché. Shots of the couple boarding their flight are disrupted by jump-cuts to stock footage of airplanes crossing the tarmac, corrupting the smooth continuity of their journey home and disrupting any sense of closure the solving of the crime may have provided. The couple smiles and laughs and the voice of psychiatrist Professor Rinaldi provides a jarring juxtaposition as he narrates his absurd explanation of the killer's psychosis. As the couple seats themselves on the plane opposite a nun, Sam's voice-over narration ironically affirms the interpretation of Italy he first arrived with: "I can hear him saying it now. Go to Italy. It's a peaceful country. Nothing ever happens there."

5

The Most Unnatural Kind of Death

IN THE FIRST SHOT OF DARIO Argento's *Opera* (1987), a reflection of the gilded interior of Parma's Teatro Regio appears in the gleaming lens of a raven's eye. The glassy image of an orchestra rehearsing Giuseppe Verdi's 1847 opera *Macbeth* flickers; the abstracted blinking eye reproduces the effect of a camera's shutter, activating our consciousness of the photographic apparatus and signaling the film's obsession with watching and witnessing, recognition and misrecognition. The articulation of this preoccupation makes us astutely aware that the film knows we are there. From this impossible perspective, the film looks back at us.

The eye is a staple motif of the horror genre. In films from *Un Chien Andalou* (1929) to *Hostel* (2005), this violation is called up as one of the most extreme cinema has to offer. As Linda Ruth Williams points out, "Damage done to eyes recurs as a symbol of the worst possible violence, a spectacular last straw in horror far more disturbing even than representations of fatal injuries to vital organs" (14). It is not surprising, then, that Argento's close-ups of opera singer Betty (Christina Marsillach), bound and gagged with rows of needles taped under her eyes, have become *Opera*'s most recognized images. But Argento uses this trope to also set up a complex system of identification, where point-of-view shots enable the audience to identify with Betty, simultaneously passive and complicit, as she watches a series of gruesome murders take place before her.

This scenario has been approached as both upholding and transgressing the generic norms of the horror genre, but it is not often considered in terms of its peculiar artificiality. The extreme violence implied by this loaded trope obscures the fact that Betty's eyes are imprisoned by needles that are not able to pierce her eyelids at all; in an extreme close-up slipped between the alternating point of view shots of Betty and the killer, it is clear that the needles taped to her cheekbone are too short to have drawn the blood that drips theatrically down her cheek. This elaborately fabricated representation of violence plays with the audience's senses of limitation and confrontation: the killer's clumsy application of the used and reused needle-lined tape looks as if it could come unstuck at any moment, but it works, cinematically, on two levels. It produces the shock that is associated with the inferred violence of the scenario, and it is also a manifestation of the *giallo* genre's predilection for self-conscious, unbounded artifice.

Such moments in the *giallo* film are often understood under the rubric of "excess." In her 1981 book on Sergei Eisenstein's *Ivan the Terrible* (1944), Kristin Thompson describes an approach to analysis that aims to account for this filmic material that escapes a film's identifiable unifying structures. She writes:

> The minute a viewer begins to notice style for its own sake or watch works which do not provide such thorough motivation, excess comes forward and must affect narrative meaning. Style is the use of repeated techniques which become *characteristic*

Figure 5.1. Eyewitness by design: Opera singer Betty (Christina Marsillach) is bound, gagged, and forced to watch the brutal set-piece murders in Dario Argento's *Opera* (1987). Digital frame enlargement.

of the work; these techniques are foregrounded so that the spectator will notice them and create connections between their individual uses. Excess does not equal style, but the two are closely linked because they both involve the material aspects of the film. Excess forms no specific patterns which we could say are characteristic of the work. But the formal organization provided by style does not exhaust the material of the filmic techniques, and a spectator's attention to style might well lead to a noticing of excess as well. (132)

The process of noticing elements or moments of excess in *giallo* films is described across fan, journalistic, and scholarly writing on the *giallo*, where almost every response—whether critical or celebratory—touches on some aspect of the films' evocation of a sense of "too much." For James Gracey, this quality is evident in Argento's work when "logic is lost in a constant bombardment of extravagance and perversely alluring stylistics" (11). Tim Brayton of *Antagony and Ecstasy* writes, "Instead of a coherent mystery narrative, *Black Belly of the Tarantula* has style by the bucketful." Vincent Canby's review of *Deep Red* also make use of the "bucket" as a motif of abundance and heavy-handedness in *giallo* movies, where Argento's film is described as a "bucket of ax-murder-movie clichés thoroughly soaked in red paint." Matthew Leyland sees Pupi Avati's *The House with the Laughing Windows* (1976) as "a slow-burning departure from the lurid excesses of the Italian *giallo* (slasher) tradition," thereby positioning the film as an atypical example of a genre characterized by excess. For Mikel Koven, excess is generated by the genre's reliance on the "set piece" as a kind of anti-unifying element that, according to his theory of vernacular cinema, is designed to "periodically grab its audience's attention" (126), supporting Thompson's observation that "excess is not only counternarrative; it is also counterunity" (134).

Excess might appear to emerge from the *giallo* against a number of possible unifying structures located within the text or the expectations of the spectator; classical narratives of detection, traditional narrative logic and expectations of spatial and temporal relations, or the aesthetics of violence might all be thought of as unifying structures the *giallo* routinely disrupts or overloads. Returning to the opening credits vignette of Bava's *Blood and Black Lace*, we could see the saturation of color and the seemingly unmotivated flatness of the actors' performances as elements that generate rupture within the first moments of the film. According to Thompson, if this excessive material escapes the film's unifying structures, its analysis is impossible, because "analysis implies finding relationships between devices [and] excessive elements do not form relationships, beyond those of coexistence" (134). But the *giallo*'s patterns of excess suggest more than accidental coexistence—we just need to look beyond its generic narrative structures in order to read them. As Thompson herself writes, "if one looks beyond narrative, at both the unified and the excessive elements at work on other levels, the underlying principles of the film (such as the hermeneutic code and the patterns of motivation) may become apparent" (140). What this final chapter suggests is that the *giallo* genre's engagement with the hermeneutic code is characteristically modernist.

Where the two previous chapters considered the genre's relation to the conditions of modernity, this final chapter zooms further in to explore the expression of this relation to modernity at the level of film style, where the *giallo*'s impulse towards reflexivity can be read as an extension of this tendency in its contemporary art cinema. Historically (and with few exceptions) film theory and criticism have positioned modernist cinema and the genre film at opposing poles; in the introduction to his book *Masterpieces of Modernist Cinema* for instance, Ted Perry states outright that one of the very defining qualities of modernist cinema is that it is not genre cinema (5). The first part of this chapter is thus concerned with what Susan Stanford Friedman has called "definitional excursions." A discussion of the relationship between modernity and modernism lays the groundwork for reading patterns of form in the *giallo* as modernist responses to the conditions of modernity. This is followed by a tracing of critical activity that has attempted to define what modernist cinema was/is and what it was not/is not. Much like the project of traditional genre criticism, such definitional acts "mean to fence in, to fix, and to stabilize" meaning (Friedman 497), and—as in the case of genre theory— the *giallo* genre presents a number of interesting problems for the idea of "modernist cinema" as a clearly delineated hermeneutic field.

Next, I will foreground a number of the formal strategies used in *giallo* films that have functioned for critics as markers of modernist cinema. Such patterns are found in the radical and reflexive exploration of film sound's agency, in the quality of abstraction generated across the films' form, and in the genre's obsession with the ontology of cinema itself. As with the canonized modernist film, in the *giallo* each of these broad strategies works to "make conscious the process of perception, celebrating the difficulty and duration of that experience" (Perry 7–8). The aim of this formal analysis is not to claim that *gialli* are "modernist masterpieces"—although a good number of them are excellent films.

Rather, what I hope to show is how modernist cinema has so often been equated with the canonized European art film and the notion of the "masterpiece" that other important sites of cinematic modernism have been overlooked.

What is it that these popular, yet often marginalized, films are doing with modernism, then? The chapter will undertake one final critical shift in exploring a possibility that can be realized only through the lens of modernist cinema: that the *giallo* genre imagines its own late-modern dystopia, where its flourishes and "excess" can be read as manifestations of decadence, and where the *giallo* genre's pessimism, boredom, and sense of decay articulate modernity's own fin de siècle moment. Conceptualizing the *giallo* film in this way renders it as a trace—an artefact from the moment right before the collapse of modernity.

Definitional Exclusions: From Modernity to Modernism

As Koven's book *La Dolce Morte* shows us, it is straightforward enough to show how *giallo* films are concerned with the conditions of modernity, but to think of them in terms of modernism presents a riskier conceptual leap. What is the difference? Rodrigues and Garrett explain that modernism can be most easily distinguished from modernity by the latter's preoccupation with new technologies or those technologies that emerged during, and as a result of, the industrial revolution. These are the technologies that build and animate the modern cities of the detective narrative: forms of transport such as trains, cars, and airplanes; new means of communication such as photography, the X-ray, the telephone, and cinema. The modern city is assembled with the new materials of reinforced concrete, plastic, and man-made fibers; it is brought to life by new sources of power and energy—particularly electricity and petroleum. According to Rodrigues and Garrett, this proliferation of new technologies works to shape the conditions of the modern world, where "the 20th century Western inhabitant speeds into totally new spheres—geographical, but also interpersonal, emotional, and cultural" (45). The ways the *giallo* film, as an artefact of the late-modern moment, interrogates these spheres of modern experience have been the principal concerns of our discussion so far.

Modernism, on the other hand, typically defines a particular set of artistic responses—in literature, music, or art—to the conditions of modernity. Characterized by such features as aesthetic self-consciousness, stylistic fragmentation, and a questioning of representation, modernist texts bear "a highly ambivalent and often critical relationship to the process of modernization" (Felski 12–13). This relationship grows from the modern's critical relationship to the classical: as András Kovács writes, "Modernism creates new values through its dispute with the classical. Modernism does not value the new simply for being new; rather, it originated in a critical-reflexive relationship with tradition. Thus modernism simultaneously affirms and negates continuity with tradition" (13). It is this dialectical relationship between tradition and the classical that leads Malcolm Bradbury and James McFarlane to call modernism "the one art that responds to the scenario of our chaos" (27). As the previous chapters have suggested, the *giallo* film is highly invested in responding to the conditions of modernity. But to call the *giallo* film modernist cinema is to undertake a critical shift that unearths two problems—and both are played out on definitional grounds.

First, the relationship between modernity and modernism is not as clear cut as some definitions of the terms might suggest. As Rodrigues and Garrett point out, the project of modernism is not simply a "kneejerk reaction to modernity" (27). The movement cannot be defined via a clearly delineated period, or through a medium specificity that prescribes use of the new forms of technologies so often linked with modernity. Modernist art is not only made from modern technologies. Perhaps most significantly, however, modernism as a project is never only interested in reproducing the processes of modernization and modernity at an aesthetic level: as Rodrigues and Garrett explain, through its use of particular techniques, modernist art "doesn't simply reflect, but also sets itself against, modernity" (5). In other words, we can consider how the progression of the *giallo* film's narrative characteristically relies on modern forms of transportation, but this alone does not mean that *giallo* films are modernist.

Similarly, many *giallo* films could fit easily into one or more of the three categories developed by Kovács to describe the types of stories late modernist films are typically interested in. Explaining that the identification of particular formal aspects alone is not enough to define late cinematic modernism, Kovács contends that "three general thematic frameworks recur in modern films":

1. disconnection of the individual human being from the environment, commonly called alienation;

2. subjective, mythological, and conceptual redefinition of the concept of reality; and

3. disclosure of the idea of nothingness behind the surface reality. (203)

Although Kovács develops these three broad thematic templates in relation to the European art film, reading the *giallo*'s engagement with modernity through these frameworks is particularly productive. Alongside their preoccupation with the conditions of modernity, *giallo* films symptomatically display the aesthetic self-consciousness, stylistic fragmentation, and questioning of representation that signify the critically reflexive relationship with tradition that defines modernism. Although they do not feature in canons of modernist cinema, by using film form to critique—and to set themselves against—modernity, *giallo* films are employing the mechanics of modernism found in the most highly canonized examples of cinematic modernism.

The concept of a "modernist canon" calls to the second problem unearthed by this critical shift: that is, a definitional battle around which texts qualify as legitimate expressions of modernism. Despite its films exhibiting many of the characteristics critics have associated with modernist cinema, the *giallo* genre presents a complicated case precisely because of its status as a genre. Perry provides us with an illustrative example. In his attempt to define what modernist cinema might be, he lays out a set of characteristics he sees as belonging to a range of films that have been critically considered as modernist texts:

> We can begin to describe the modernist film by suggesting what it is not. It is not a genre film. If the genre film is formulaic, one whose conventions are shared by filmmaker and audience, the modernist film is one without conventions. The genre film is intuitively recognized as familiar, similar to a whole group of films, but the modernist film is unfamiliar. (5)

In this view, the audience's presumed familiarity with the conventions of the genre film disqualifies such films from being considered legitimate modernist texts, presumably because what is described as the "unfamiliar" helps to facilitate the rupture of audience expectation so often associated with the logic of the modernist film.

However, there are three points at which this distinction between modernist and genre cinema begins to dissolve. Such definitions typically do not take into account the fact that the system of genre relies as much on difference as it does on repetition in terms of meaning-making processes. That is, the genre film perpetually strives both to cultivate and rupture the viewer's expectations. While this dialectic may sometimes produce the sense of familiarity Perry associates with the genre film, it also endows the system of genre with the ability to break through the viewer's preconstituted expectations and hypotheses. Secondly, the proposition that the modernist film has no conventions while the genre film is only ever familiar reveals how such definitions rely on particular assumptions about the spectator as a fixed, homogenous, and ahistorical subject. By adopting a diachronic approach to the investigation of the *giallo* genre, this book has suggested (particularly in chapter 2) how the constitution and understanding of genre are always historically contingent and subjectively understood, thus destabilizing any universal notion of what is conventional to the film spectator and what is not. Finally, this distinction does not allow for the possibility of a genre that is fundamentally concerned with the inherent tension of late modernity and responds to it using the stylistic characteristics of canonized modernist form.

Perry's definitional introduction to *Masterpieces of Modernist Cinema* demonstrates the category's typical mapping and its critical boundaries; such definitional accounts of this liquid canon are simultaneously broad (to account for some difference between the wide range of films typically included) and limiting, in that they categorically refuse membership to particular types, such as the genre film. One paradigm set up to arrive at "useful definitions" of the modernist film is to imagine a continuum where "purely graphic and abstract filmmaking" lies at one end, while "pleasurable and informative" cinema such as narrative films and documentaries lie at the other. The distance between the poles of this continuum has to do with the viewer's conscious perception of realism, with the abstract films having "no resemblance to nature" while the films at the opposite pole function in line with our idea of what's realistic (even if we understand them as constructs) (1–2). Perry goes on to explain how,

> in the middle of our continuum, where modernist films exist, there is a point where abstraction and realism meet. All of the films discussed in this volume work this threshold between the purely realistic and the purely abstract, never wholly either.

> With two exceptions . . . the essays in this book demonstrate how some individual films utilize a diversity of impulses and tactics to undermine the purely abstract and purely realistic gravitational pulls at the extremes of this continuum. The films chosen . . . embody the major strategies used by modernist filmmakers. (2)

In order to arrive at a useful taxonomy of modernist cinema, Perry then lists some of the dominant and recurrent formal patterns such "modernist masterpieces" exhibit, which map some of the typical critical biases that preclude genre cinema from speaking to discourses of modernism. In attempting to delineate modernist cinema Perry offers a number of somewhat vague markers: modernist films are described as "singular," or films that characteristically oppose the concept of genre, and are often texts that only make sense to some viewers (6–7). More quantifiable might be Perry's claim that one of the key identifying tropes of modernist cinema is its use of reflexivity: a mode where "the space between screen and viewer is animated by the viewer's consciousness of watching the film" (7). Although this reflexive tendency is foregrounded in most critical considerations of modernist cinema, the identification and definition of this complex characteristic have produced their own complex history.

In 1971, the same year Cavara's *giallo* film *The Black Belly of the Tarantula* was released, Thomas Elsaesser's critique of *le direct* acknowledged cinema's potential to "appeal to intelligence and the senses." His aim was to unpack particular elitist attitudes to narrative cinema, but his recognition of its ability to "develop an inner dialectic"—between intellect and spectacle—is also key to understanding how reflexivity in the *giallo* film is able to interrogate the ontology of cinema as rigorously as the most canonized modernist European art film. From our privileged position of critical and historical distance, the focus of *le direct*'s ideological project—developed in reaction to a traditional and mainstream cinema—grows cloudy and more complex. Those hallmark tropes of self-consciousness and reflexivity that become so tightly bound to European art cinema through the work of film criticism surface now not only in what Elsaesser calls "an uncompromisingly hermetic avant-garde" (3), but in its contemporary popular cinema, too.

This dialectic is the site for my final rehearsal of the problems that arise from the definitional act's inherent dependence on the binary of inclusion and exclusion. As Friedman argues:

Definitional acts establish territories, map terrains, determine centers, margins, and areas beyond the pale. Attempts to establish permeable borderlands instead of fixed boundaries and liminal spaces of considerable intermixing between differences diffuse to some extent the territorial imperative of definition but cannot ultimately eliminate the function of categories to demarcate some phenomena in opposition to others which do not belong. As Toni Morrison writes about canon formation (a type of definitional act in literary, art, and religious history), "Canon building is Empire building. Canon defense is national defense. Canon debate, whatever the terrain, nature and range . . . is the clash of cultures. And all of the interests are vested." (506)

Just as the terrain of Italian national cinema is so often mapped with those films seen to make "valuable," and thus legitimate, contributions to the idea of the nation, the canon of modernist cinema resists absorbing films it positions as conventional or generic. These boundaries between modernist cinema and the *giallo* film are thus maintained despite common strategies and aesthetic concerns.

One site where border crossing between modernism and genre cinema has taken place is within critical consideration of film noir. William Luhr and Peter Lehman, for example, in their work on the subgenre of the police procedural, explain how "film noir, with its central trope of urban decay, of the failed utopian urban dream," becomes "a premier site for dystopian modernism" (175). While utopian modernism celebrates the modern era's new art and architecture, technological advancement, and potential for liberal class reform, dystopian modernism articulates the growing anxiety generated by the conditions of modernity. In perpetually growing cities, shadows become longer and darker, concealing new horrors reflected in skyrocketing crime rates. The achievements and progress of the modern era take on a new ambiguity as individuals are increasingly disconnected from a sense of community amidst a rapidly expanding space.

Luhr and Lehman find in the police procedural a combination of utopian and dystopian strains of modernism, where the utopian potential of new crime-fighting technologies is showcased in dystopian cities where the world of crime flourishes and expands. What Luhr and Lehman see as an "odd and at times contradictory" (177) amalgam of utopian and dystopian strains of modernism recalls the contradictory messages Koven sees as embodied in the genre's celebration of the glossy, jet-set lifestyles of its characters and the design-heavy modern aesthetic of their world, while it simultaneously plots to kill them off, one by one. But the tension produced by such contradictions is itself a condition of modernity.

For Raymond Bellour, these ambiguities, tensions, and contradictions are precisely where modernism is located in genre film texts; in his 1966 essay "Sur Fritz Lang," Bellour aims to develop a "systematic approach to the Langian universe" that accounts for the ways Lang's genre cinema speaks through modernist strategies (28). The loaded ambiguity Bellour celebrates in Lang's films is the same quality Perry sees in the masterpieces of modernist cinema: the "fascination and difficulty one experiences in watching [Lang's] films" (29); an "intensified partialization of space" (31); and a "flagrant and deliberately abstract waiting" or "disequilibrium" (32), which he finds in all of Lang's work. This analysis of Lang leads Bellour to conclude that the genre director can be best understood not through the regularity of systems, but through the "fissures . . . the gaps which he sets up" (33). He describes how,

> as [Lang] strains the shot and unbalances it, he loses sight of his narrative, obscuring his characters. And thus he works . . . in counter-genre; even in America, he simultaneously espouses and insidiously transgresses the laws of the most traditional art. He incorporates the principle and destroys it. (33)

In celebrating Lang's capacity to simultaneously uphold and violate the rules of classical filmmaking, Bellour describes an approach to reading Lang's film noirs that foregrounds waiting and disequilibrium as crucial elements of the work. Although Bellour is concerned with Lang in particular, these dynamics he describes are central to the film noir genre more broadly, as well as the *giallo* genre, where in the late-modern context they become key tropes.

Similarly, Luhr and Lehman explain how, in the case of film noir, a sense of anxiety is recuperated into the genre, fusing with other genre elements to become a key generic expectation. For Luhr and Lehman, this is "an anxiety that exists on a different plane from that of responses to disturbing places, characters, and activities in individual films because it is associated with the genre itself" (178). The authors cite "representational strategies, destabilizing techniques, and even reception contexts," which fashion the world of the film noir as the troubling and alienating locale we know it to be (179). When this destabilization and sense of anxiety begin to emanate from the genre itself, key characteristics of modernist cinema are being perpetuated through the system of genre. The *giallo* genre works similarly with the tropes of modernist cinema to produce its own peculiar and violent world. However, if, as Luhr and Lehman argue, film noir's anxiety is produced through insinuation of what lies beyond the frame—or through the obscure and unrepresentable—the late modern *giallo* world reveals a schism that lies beyond every imaginable transgression. On the eve of the collapse of modernity, these films no longer gesture towards the inescapable void: it is reflected, indefinitely, in a pool of blood.

Destabilization of Spatial and Temporal Order

The *giallo* film routinely challenges the cinematic pleasures of classical narrative by breaking down or through spatial and temporal logic. One device Argento in particular employs to this end is the vignette sequence. In one of *Deep Red*'s most memorable sequences, the director's camera pans over a series of inanimate objects that are laid out on a smooth, black surface. As we glide ominously over a paper doll's crib, it is knocked over with a glass marble that rolls into frame; we then pass over a woolen doll pierced with sewing pins; more violent children's drawings, of the kind we encounter elsewhere in the film, and various pieces of plaited twine. We examine in close-up a silver statuette embellished with colored stones. The camera holds still for a moment and a black leather–gloved hand picks up a tiny, naked plastic doll, before gliding over a cluster of glass marbles, a red plastic demon figure, and, finally, a selection of menacing knives.

These ominous shots float above the surface of the narrative, unbound from decipherable context or true sense of motivation. There is no indication of place or even space; no walls or doors to anchor the spectator spatially in the diegesis. Are we in the killer's imagination, or subconscious? Does this deranged selection of objects provide some clue to the killer's identity or to the mystery at hand? We do not know and it does not matter, because the purpose of the shots is not to progress the narrative. The camera's intense fetishization of the various objects renders them less as clues and more as specimens of various colors and textures, laid out for its—and our—roving interrogation. Such a moment seems, by Thompson's definition, to be a textbook example of the type of "excess" that emerges when "certain props carry interest beyond their function in the narrative" (521). But there is also an alternative logic at work here, where the film becomes—for the duration of the vignette—an experimental meditation on the camera's ability to capture the reflective circumference of a child's colored glass marbles or the abrasive and fibrous texture of a woolen doll.

Being asked to "look" is one way the *giallo* film expresses its self-consciousness, and something it asks us to look at with regularity is stylized violence. As is the case with any genre, the spectatorial experience offered by *giallo* film's violence depends fundamentally on the level of familiarity with the generic code. Leo Braudy writes that for fan audiences highly literate in generic conventions the function and effect of violence can change: "The audience's knowledge of genre convention, like its awareness of sequels and remakes, helps perform the same function as a funeral service does for mourners: turning discomfort, fear, and anxiety into matters of ritual, elegance, and even routine" (223). Violence in the *giallo* film is one of the rituals performed to display membership to a particular body of films. Much of the aesthetic intensity of *Deep Red*, for instance, is realized in the film's moments of extreme violence, when the operatic performance of brutality is stretched and extended into abstraction. These rituals of violence are devices that allow the films to explore the medium's specificity by generating spaces where color, texture, and movement work experimentally to create a more primary aesthetic pleasure than the extreme violence might first indicate. But violence is also an important device to facilitate the fragmentation of the body and the destabilization of spatial and temporal order.

Often, we are positioned to misrecognize what we see. In *Opera*, Mira (Daria Nicolodi) is punished for peeping and Betty is forced to watch, but in *Deep Red*, Marcus finds himself embroiled in the film's increasingly bizarre case precisely because he does not recognize what he has witnessed. This self-consciousness at the level of narrative has been cited as a recurring trope of the genre, but the films work through this preoccupation with spectatorship and voyeurism through mise-en-scène and form too. In *Deep Red*, the voyeuristic act of film spectatorship is simulated not only through shots that take the killer's point-of-view, but also through repeated extreme close-up shots of the killer's eye. At the home of novelist and victim Amanda Righetti (Giuliana Calandra), a quick zoom into the blackness of an open cupboard reveals a single eye that opens suddenly and looks from left to right, disembodied and floating in the pitch darkness. In another instance, during a close-up shot of the murderer maniacally outlining her eyes in black kohl, the camera begins to ominously spiral in a clockwise 360-degree spin. This concentric circle formation (on which the Spanish film poster capitalizes) recalls the key images of both Hitchcock's *Vertigo* (1958) and Bigas Luna's *Anguish* (1987), in which spiral motifs become symbols for disorientation and fragmentation. This formation is echoed through the movement of the camera at other points in the film too, such as when Marcus returns to the site of the first crime in order to try to piece together what has happened. As he stands on the street, looking up at Helga Ulmann's (Macha Méril) apartment, the camera sweeps around from behind, encircling him as he fails to comprehend the logic of what he has witnessed.

The stylized fragmentation of the body is a representational technique that can be found across the genre too, beyond its violent set pieces. Think of the unnervingly voyeuristic tilted close-ups on Ewa Aulin's face in Questi's *Death Laid an Egg*, or the way light carves characters' bodies into slices in Lado's *Short Night of Glass Dolls*. The fragmentation of the body is matched by a persistent formal discontinuity that works hard to maintain disequilibrium through the abstraction of both time and space. Through this formal discontinuity, the social disconnection experienced by the inhabitants of the *giallo* world is relentlessly expressed at the level of style. Perry alludes to this as a quality of the modernist film when he writes that,

> in many of the modernist films, there is either no sense of where the film is going and how it will end, or there is a conception of cause and effect that is foreign to most narratives.

Figure 5.2. Reporter Gregory Moore (Jean Sorel) plays detective in Aldo Lado's *Short Night of Glass Dolls* (1971). Digital frame enlargement.

While the entertainment film often makes us comfortable with a clear point of view and structure, the modernist film is more likely to challenge such cinematic pleasures. (7)

The *giallo* can also celebrate difficulty through its manipulation of temporality. As the vignette from *Deep Red* illustrates, the relationship between plot time and story time can be particularly obtuse. In other *gialli*, this relationship is configured to foreground discontinuity in a way that provides an absolute rupture. *The Pyjama Girl Case* (Flavio Mogherini, 1977) provides an illustrative example, where disruptive editing often has characters continue lines of dialogue in completely new locations, jolting the spectator out of any comfort in narrative and spatial logic. These jarring edits are initially correlated with a number of narrative "hooks," but as the film progresses the relationship between these strategies weakens to the point of disillusion. The conclusion reveals the key to the film's alienating temporality: we have been watching both the past and the present scrambled, but the lack of suspense generated through the film's alienating style renders the final "twist" redundant, only emphasizing the constructedness of the film. The film's disruptive editing style is highlighted in a 1978 *Variety* review, where the critic writes that it weakens "an already feeble script to the point that the story is confused, verging on the unintelligible. The relationship between the love affair and the murder is obscure until the very end. Thus, tension and suspense build up continuously, only to be interrupted and dissipated by the flashbacks" (Ancy 34). When contextualized by the pattern of disruptive temporalities in *giallo* films more broadly, however, Mogherini's film can be seen to offer a variation of this pervasive tendency.

The zoom represents another fundamentally reflexive formal device often used in *giallo* films as a force of disruption. Unlike tracking shots, in which the camera itself moves, the sense of movement achieved by the zoom is the product of the lens' focal length changing during the single take. In a tracking shot, perspective changes as the camera moves through space, but with the zoom perspective is maintained, creating an uneasy sensation of impossible movement. The speed at which the focal length shifts in the typical *giallo* zoom recalls the quick rate of optical magnification achieved through the use of optical instruments such as the telescope or binoculars; as John Belton writes, "The zoom lens is not really normal. It is a bionic, not a human, eye" (23). Paul Willemen points out that throughout the 1960s and early 1970s the zoom became "a constant and rhetorical feature in films by the likes of Jesus Franco and Mario Bava" that could be read as an emphatic instance of authorial presence (106). The zoom causes what Koven characterizes as a "lens disruption that is abrupt and jarring, certainly not the smooth transition favored by the continuity system" (150). Within Koven's theory of vernacular cinema, the zoom shot cues the *giallo*'s vernacular audience to the significance of the following shot, but in many *giallo* films the zoom shots command more attention than the shots that bookend them (155). Take, for instance, the frequent zooms in Carnimeo's *The Case of the Bloody Iris*, which repeatedly hurtle the viewer towards actor Edwige Fenech's deep brown, heavily made-up eyes.

In his essay on boredom and Umberto Lenzi's *Spasmo* (1974), Chris Fujiwara suggests a more nuanced function of the zoom shot. He explains how the director of *Spasmo*

> uses the zoom as punctuation, marking the start and end of shots with emphasis; to give structure to his scenes, to give the semblance of movement to dialogues and shapes that lack inner movement: not just the actors who pretend to be corpses . . . but also the actors who pretend to be alive but are unable to supply inner movement. The zoom compensates for, but also confirms and celebrates, the tendency of characters in *Spasmo* to become inanimate and doll-like. (249)

Although his case study is a single film, Fujiwara points out that the zoom lens and its characteristic function of drawing attention to the artifice of the film text surfaces right across the broad range of genre production in the Italian commercial cinema of the period:

> As in other products of the Italian cinematic system, the zoom in *Spasmo* constitutes the characters as static visual patterns. The zoom controls an extended space, but the animate creatures who occupy this space are immobile or suspended, or their movement is annulled: exterior movement is held in abeyance while the movement of consciousness is performed by the zoom. (248)

As I have argued elsewhere, it may be the *giallo* film's characters who experience this movement of consciousness facilitated by the zoom when suspects are glimpsed from a distance and suddenly recognized (*Deep Red*). But very often, the zoom is indicative of the movement of our own consciousness. The zoom in Bava's *Five Dolls for an August Moon* that fragments the corpse of Fenech's character Marie, does so by refocusing our attention to the knife protruding from her torso with a level of abstraction no character in the diegesis could experience. In this moment, as Belton suggests, the zoom shot "reflects a way of seeing the world not as it appears to the human eye, but, perhaps, as it really is" (27). Fujiwara also points out that the stasis achieved by the zoom shot is not only a disruption of space, but an annulment of time. In this respect, he links the prevalence of the zoom shot in *giallo* films to their characteristic use of the car as a motif. Suggesting that the *giallo* film's use of both the zoom and the car renders them "technologies of imaginary possession" (249), Fujiwara reminds us that the frequent motor travel in *giallo* films typically presents opportunities for montages of travelogue-type scenery that are characteristically excessive in terms of their frequent lack of significant motivation. These often-banal sequences disrupt previously established rhythm or tempo and, through their blatant discontinuity, draw attention to the films' constructedness.

Music and Sound as Forces of Disruption

In her essay "Troubling Synthesis," Kay Dickinson makes the observation that, where the Italian horror film has attracted the attention of the academy, it has been primarily in relation to aesthetics and visual style. But music and sound have played significant roles in the cultivation of the *giallo* genre's reputation—particularly in cult cinema discourses—as a film genre associated with style. Dickinson brings this oversight to our attention to propose that the synth-driven soundtracks of a number of Italian video nasties, including Argento's *Tenebrae* (1982), in fact played an active role in the titles' banning under the Video Recordings Act of 1984. While Kate Egan's work on the video nasties convincingly suggests that it was extratextual material such as video cover artwork, as well as promotional and marketing material, that played the most significant role in this censorship panic (*Trash or Treasure*), Dickinson's hypothesis makes an interesting point about the function of music in these films that challenges traditional approaches to the relationship between sound and image in cinema. From Goblin's renowned work on *Deep Red* to the slinky stylized *giallo* scores of Bruno Nicolai and Morricone, the *giallo* film soundtrack is a key site for the genre's sense of disruption and self-consciousness.

In the first post-vignette scene in *Deep Red*, Lithuanian telepathist Helga Ulmann sits before the audience of a parapsychology conference in Rome, writhing and struggling with a "twisted mind" who is sending her "perverted, murderous thoughts." She looks out beyond the audience, pointing, and stammers, "You . . . have killed. And you will kill again." The terror in her voice is palpable and yet her lips move at a more languid pace that is at odds with the rhythm of her urgent warning. The voice dubbing in *Deep Red* is out of sync here and this only adds to the mysterious quality of Helga's unsettling premonition. As Antje Ascheid argues, the practices of postproduction sound and voice dubbing remain relatively undertheorized in terms of their impact on the film text. In critical literature that does acknowledge this impact, one can detect a general consensus regarding the practices' ability to annihilate the "quality" of the original text. In "The Cinema after Babel," Ella Shochat and Robert Stam investigate the effects of subtitling and dubbing, explaining how dubbing, in particular, leads to "a number of anomalous situations," including the use of unfamiliar voices to dub known actors, generating a rupture or "irritant" for the audience (50). The fundamental problem with voice dubbing as they see it, regards the flattening out of cultural specificity that the practice achieves. Where subtitling allows for the preservation of the original voice track alongside the translated text, for Shochat and Stam dubbing deletes any aural trace of the original voice track, systematically denying its condition as a translated text: "To graft one language, with its own system of linking sound and gesture, onto the visible behaviour associated with another, then, is to foster a kind of cultural violence and dislocation" (52). Despite their admission that the original film text has no claim to "purity," Shochat and Stam characterize the process of dubbing as one that "results in a kind of monstrosity" (52). These monstrous texts that are unable to remark on the culture that produces them reinforces the dominance of a hegemonic language—and in the case of subsequent audiences of the *giallo*, this is most often English.

Ascheid takes issue with this interpretation of dubbing and its effects, showing how the dubbed film text might work in more complex ways than generally understood. For Ascheid, the dubbed film is an entirely new and "fundamentally recontextualized" artefact constructed through this process: "Consequently, the employment of dubbing as a translation technique must be seen as transforming the original into a blueprint, which shifts its status from that of a finished and culturally specific text to that of a transcultural denationalized raw material, which is to be reinscribed into a new cultural context via the dubbing process" (33).

Because both the production and reception contexts of the *giallo* have meant that the films already have a particularly transcultural identity, it is fitting to see the dubbing process as another manifestation of this constant recontextualization. To position the films in this way opens up (at least) two ways of reading the dubbing of *giallo* films productively.

Firstly, the English-language dub track could be contextualized as part of the manufactured, hegemonic sense of anyplace that Baschiera and Di Chiara describe in their article on the transnational features of Italian genre film production in the 1960s and 1970s. The context of genre film production during this period provides numerous sites for transnational qualities to emerge, from the use of non-Italian actors and settings to the typical use of foreign characters in the films' narratives. Rather than flattening out cultural specificity, these qualities, along with the use of dubbing, recontextualize the spaces in which *giallo* films are shot and conjure a new and ambiguous culture. For the genre's subsequent, non-Italian, audiences, dubbing registers as a key stylistic and aesthetic marker of the genre. When encountered by cultures that more often subtitle foreign language films, the practice of dubbing works to *maintain* a sense of cultural specificity, which can be read as an Italian sensibility in particular.

More interesting, however, is how the uneven quality of voice dubbing serves to further expose the artifice of the cinematic text, by disrupting the synchronicity that reinforces the illusion of traditional narrative cinema. As Fuijiwara points out in his essay on boredom and Umberto Lenzi's film *Spasmo* (1974):

> It may be more accurate to say of the Italian system that it tolerates as no breach of verisimilitude a somewhat greater obvious discrepancy between voice and image than is usually acceptable in the cinemas of the United States, Britain, or France, that it tolerates disruption between sound and image and the presence of traces of the independence of sound from image (e.g., obviously inexact lip synching) to a greater extent than do other cinematic systems. (252)

In this sense, dubbing participates in the disruption and fragmentation that pervade the films more broadly.

However, reflexivity at play in the *giallo* soundtrack does not only surface as a result of industrial process and historical distance. The genre already uses sound as a site for self-conscious exploration of the cinema as a plastic art. In their introduction to *Beyond the Soundtrack: Representing Music in Cinema*, Goldmark, Kramer, and Leppert speculate on the possible reasons for critics' and theorists' marginalization of film music. One suggestion is that "perhaps the dominance of the image in our understanding of film is a reflection of the traditional association of knowing with seeing" (2). If this is the case, it follows that the *giallo* genre's fascination with the ambiguous relationship between seeing and knowing flags a particular and unusual use of music in the genre. In his book on reflexivity, Stam suggests that the function of film music is to "charm the spectator into forgetting the passage of time" (168), describing the musical score that guides the spectator's emotional response to the images the film presents, to condemn or justify particular action taking place. Motifs are associated with particular characters to signal arrival and departure, or propose narrative cues regarding the relations between characters. In the traditional narrative cinema, the score works in service to the image and the purpose of the musical score in the orthodox film is fundamentally illusionist.

But the nondiegetic musical soundtrack of the *giallo* film rarely functions in this simple accentual fashion. More typically, music—both diegetic and nondiegetic scores—are dynamic agents of aesthetic self-consciousness. Halfway through *Deep Red*, for instance, we find protagonist Marcus sitting at the piano in his Rome apartment, working on a new composition. Trialing a new motif in ascending keys, the camera watches him mark notation onto his manuscript with fluency and precision, and follows his hand across the page with a phantasmagoric pan in extreme close-up. The next shot reveals the advancement of the killer, whose slow, rhythmic pace keeps time with the pianist's experimentation. The ascending motif is used here in a conventional way to build tension and suspense around the scene, but the effect is a consequence of the reflexive scenario set up by Argento, where the diegetic music Marcus plays comments on the action of the killer whom he cannot see.

Soon additional music is heard in the diegesis, when a song new to Marcus, but familiar to *Deep Red*'s audience, begins to echo through the apartment. This haunting children's song from the film's opening vignette emanates from a tape recorder that the killer brings to her own crime scene. Later, Professor Giordanni self-consciously refers to the song as "the leitmotif of the crimes." Although the killer carries her own musical motif to her intended crime scenes, the tape recorder itself is never contextualized by appearing in this space: instead, it floats in close-up as the killer's black-gloved finger presses the play button. When Daly plays his recording of the killer's motif to the professor, Argento revisits the motif of "sound writing" through an extreme close-up of the turntable's stylus as it traces the vinyl in concentric circles. Like the spinning eye of the killer, this stylized flourish spirals us deeper into the film's reflexive center, pushing us further into the unorthodox viewing experience Perry aligns with modernist cinema.

Like the film's diegetic sound, the Goblin score for *Deep Red* has a supernatural level of agency as part of the film's structure. In the lengthy and visually stunning sequence that follows Marcus around the abandoned, baroque house that Argento has linked to the children's song, the nondiegetic component of the film's soundtrack dictates how the sequence unfolds diegetically. As Marcus pushes open the ostentatious art nouveau iron gate to the property, the entrance—like those of so many of its cinematic predecessors—offers an obligatory creak of warning. But as he stands at the entrance contemplating his best course of action, a sparse, repetitive, and bass-driven refrain begins to snake about the scene. Meandering through the grand, dusty house, Daly seems propelled by the pulsating bass, punctuated with dashes of tingling, shimmering cymbals and tiny cracks of the snare. When he steps on some broken glass, the music stops, momentarily flipping the traditional balance of power between image and sound in the cinema. When he moves to open a window to let in more light and a curtain rod falls to the floor, the sound prompts the return of the responsive bass line, reestablishing the sense that the nondiegetic score watches the image from above, teases it, and dares its protagonist to go on looking. At the top of the stairs, the telltale pounding of a heartbeat pushes the score aside, signaling that he is close to finding a clue. Although he cannot hear the sound, the pulsation of this terrible heart draws Marcus to the wall that, under layers of paint and plaster, hides a naive illustration of the opening vignette. The score in this sequence is so driven that it gives the impression of necessitating the sequence in the first place—as if the score has conjured the image in order to have something to play with. The soundtrack's unorthodox behavior in *Deep Red* offers one example of how *giallo* films use film sound to draw attention to the plasticity of film.

Other *gialli* demonstrate a less cohesive relation between these filmic elements. In these cases, the *giallo* score is loosely tied to the narrative and visual fabrics of the films, resulting in a relationship characterized by the dominance of disruption and fissure. The characteristics of this relation suggest that the musical soundtrack is "thrown over" the visual and narrative elements of the film; like those soundtracks that Dickinson describes, these scores refuse to make suitable moral comment on the (often violent) images they accompany. But the effect they produce might be even more complex. In his essay on the beauty of supermarket music, Joseph Lanza writes about a kind of film music that has a "blanketing effect": this is film music that functions like supermarket music—music designed to be heard, not listened to (1995). But this easy "blanket" application of film music is something that Lanza questions. Lanza uses the phenomenon of Muzak to demonstrate how what we see and hear simultaneously are always connected in some significant way. Listening in the supermarket, he considers the possibility of a shopper recognizing a familiar tune used by the background Muzak. This scenario generates the possibility for multiple connections between visual and sonic experience that extend beyond the intended design of the Muzak that is playing. That is, the audience's recognition of familiar songs in Muzak versions and their subsequent recollection of original version lyrics, has the potential to overturn the intended effect of this "nondescript" music. At the same time, the listener is reflexively aware of the Muzak as a reference that points to elsewhere, that draws attention to its own (re)construction.

Using this example of alternative identification with sound, Lanza unpacks the ambivalence of "blanketed" music to illuminate the possibilities of it producing meaning. Likewise, listening closely to the *giallo* score reveals how the sonic dynamics of the cinema do not merely accent or ignore the other filmic elements; nor do they simply look in the other direction while people are being killed. The *giallo* film score articulates its own dislocation from the image and narrative in more extreme ways than Muzak: unlike the lobotomized, sweetened versions of well-known songs that make up supermarket music, music in *gialli* is most often score written specifically for the film. It frequently employs the female voice as a kind of ethereal instrument that sings wordless melodic lines, dampening the possibility of lyrical associations or recognition. But it maintains and advances the modernist questioning of representation happening at the level of image in the *giallo*, by drawing attention to itself as a filmic element in dispute with the classical.

A fine example of this strategy can be heard in the sequence surrounding Marie's death in Mario Bava's *Five Dolls for an August Moon*. In this 1973 *giallo*, friends enjoying a relaxing holiday in a luxury house on a secluded island begin to suspect each other of murder when one of their party turns up dead. This event marks the beginning of a series of killings that eliminate each member of the group, one by one. In this particular sequence, with two friends dead already, the holiday party is searching for their friend Jack, whom they believe is missing. Trudy and

Dick return to the living room after unsuccessfully searching the island; as Dick declines Trudy's offer of a drink, the soundtrack offers a short and jangling series of chords that alert Dick to the presence of Jack's body, slumped in a chair. Before either character or the audience, the film music knows that Jack is in the room. More than this, the characters seem to hear and respond to this nondiegetic melancholic refrain just as we do. There is a fleeting moment of relief as the full party gathers and realizes that Jack has been asleep, but when Dick asks where his wife Marie is, the camera suddenly leers to the right of screen and, moving outside, begins a nauseating spin that renders the image incomprehensible. While we are stuck on this broken merry-go-round, the melancholic organ is slammed to emit a shrill cacophony that builds in intensity and pitch until, like the jab of a knife, a thick bass line kicks in accompanied by a lazy funk drum rhythm. The image spins and spirals into madness, propelled by the film's soundtrack, and then the knife we've already heard the sonic cue for appears in close-up. The shining blade is stuck crudely in the torso of a female victim and the wound is punctuated with thick, garish blood. When the shot zooms out, we realize that this is indeed Marie, dead and tied to a tree in her underwear. But the film's soundtrack already knew this. As the shot pans right, then left, and right again, theatrically framing those remaining on the island as possible suspects, the organ delivering the melodic line is replaced with a wispy clarinet that plays

Figure 5.3. Who was where, when? Marie's (Edwidge Fenech) friends discover her corpse in Mario Bava's *Five Dolls for an August Moon* (1970). Digital frame enlargement.

in a call-and-response configuration with the twinkling of a frantically plucked harp. The melodic line that we have heard before transforms into the sonic equivalent of the 1970s polyester nightgowns worn by the female characters, translucent and arousing in their insubstantiality and melodiously erotic. The music pulls back, almost as quickly as it burst in, and George delivers an overemphasized one-liner: "This time, seltzer water won't turn the trick."

In the next shot, Maria's body, wrapped in plastic, swings to and fro on a hook in the cold room, alongside a beef carcass and her two dead friends. A piano now mimics the musical motif of the previous shot in a demented and honky-tonk saloon style, recalling the player pianos of the late nineteenth and early twentieth centuries. This tantalizingly hollow rendition recalls an instrument but no musician; the distinct sonic quality of the self-playing piano—automated, mechanic—shakes a sarcastic finger at the unfortunate players of this island game. What this sequence illuminates is the disjunction that Dickinson perceives between image and soundtrack in films like *Tenebrae* and *Cannibal Holocaust* (1980). Characterized by the violent and spectacular image accompanied by music that refuses to guide the spectator's response to that image, this is "the specially written score that refuses to reiterate a closely empathetic message about the film's action" (169). In its refusal to guide the viewer in this classical sense, however, it also disrupts the spectatorial experience in a way that is characteristic of modernist cinema.

Her Last Breath: Modernist Decadence

In exploring the complex project of defining modernity and modernism, Friedman concedes that resisting the desire to provide a new definition is difficult for the theorist: "The magnetic slide towards fixed meaning feels irresistible at times." "Instead," she writes, "I have attempted to shift attention to the processes and patterns of definitional contestation" (510). In this spirit, I wish to point to one final possible prism for reading the *giallo* film's kaleidoscopic patterns.

Although it is possible to read the stylization of film form that becomes synonymous with the *giallo* genre as modernist, it can lack the formal restraint, morality, and discipline found in more canonized examples of cinematic modernism. When he writes that, unlike the genre film, "the modernist film remains fresh," Perry stacks canonized modernist cinema's perceived continued relevance against the repetitive redundancy of the genre film. *Giallo* films do have a unique and particular resonance, but it is one of stasis, or a kind of paralysis that floats on an undercurrent of anxiety around what might come next. Like that stylus tracing the scratched record as the plate moves around and around in circles, the never-ending repetition of an anxious crackling suggests a bottomless and inescapable nothingness. Being caught in this schism is not a moment of excess or a temporary departure from a unified structure; rather, it constitutes a space unto itself that is carved out through the mechanics of the genre system.

The expression of modernism in the *giallo* film feels *decadent*. This initially derogatory term was first used to describe a group of late nineteenth-century writers including Charles Baudelaire, Theophile Gautier, and Joris-Karl Huysmans, who were influenced by symbolism and the historical gothic literary tradition, as well as the work of Edgar Allan Poe. Most significantly, the decadents were fundamentally interested in the value of artifice. Although decadence is most often thought to describe the transition between romanticism and modernism, the *giallo*'s sense of lateness and its frequent characterization as "excessive" recalls this late nineteenth-century mode in a number of important ways.

As Marion Thain notes in "Modernist *Homage* to the *Fin de Siècle*," the modernists' rejection of decadent or fin de siècle ideology and literature is well documented. However, and as Thain goes on to argue, there is a palpable connection between the two movements that writers have only recently begun to untangle. For Thain, the polarized distinction between modernism and decadence is part of a "myth of discontinuity" (22) perpetuated by writing on modernism that is "still too conditioned by the modernist's own mythology" (23). Thain cites David Weir's *Decadence and the Making of Modernism* as an example of work that offers a particularly useful paradigm for understanding the influence of the fin de siècle moment on subsequent movements by presenting "decadence as not only an age of transition in which the origins of modernism must be located, but itself inherently a 'dynamics of transition'" (Thain, 23). Further to this, Neville Morely argues that decadence "does not imply a single, unvarying trajectory towards a specified terminus" (574) and that it is the critic's frequent recourse to using evolutionary cycles as theoretical models that implies otherwise. He goes on to explain how

> "decadence" does not necessarily mark the last stage before a cycle repeats itself; it may instead be seen as the penultimate stage before a range of possible endings, or even as a beginning. It marks the moment when the future begins to come

within reach, the point where the present weakens enough to make an alternative conceivable—although of course there is little agreement among writers as to what will, or should, take its place. (574)

Weir and Morely's characterizations of decadence as "in-between" states or "a dynamics of transition" are apt descriptions of the tonality of the *giallo* film, which tends to exploit the anxiety produced by such states of liminality in a late-modern context.

The significance of liminality and thresholds to the *giallo* genre also finds a parallel with what Matthew Potolsky has described as the decadent collector's "focus on the forbidden, grotesque, or 'unnatural'" (224). Potolsky recalls the collection of rare flowers that resemble rotting flesh owned by Des Esseintes, the protagonist of J. K. Huysmans's 1884 novel *A rebours* (*Against Nature*), a man who, repulsed by his contemporary society, retreats into an ideal world of his own artistic creation. Des Esseintes's excessive collecting, collating, and celebration of artifice is reflected in the way the *giallo* genre both collects and houses decadent tropes, such as the killer's inventive and increasingly bizarre methods for killing victims. As Koven points out, a *giallo* like Argento's *Sleepless* forms its own collection of extravagant, unnatural deaths: "In addition to death by musical instrument and fountain pen, people are slashed with a knife, chopped with an axe, hanged, bashed fatally into a wall, drowned and shot" (63). In one particularly reflexive example, a victim in Lamberto Bava's *A Blade in the Dark* (1983) is strangled with a length of celluloid. As chapter two illustrates, such celebration of artifice becomes further canonized through the taste formations of the cult audience, which characteristically lauds the genre's theatrical violence, celebrating its prosthetics and special effects as an art form.

Potolsky also makes the point that Des Esseintes's decadent collections are exercises in the establishment of alternative groupings that oppose the essentialism of traditional canons. The taste culture of decadence generates and houses collections that "are idiosyncratic assemblages," reflecting the description of the *giallo* genre as a hybrid form. However, as Potolsky points out, the characteristics of the decadent collection—and, by extension, the *giallo* genre—have an important political resonance in that they reflexively critique the definitional act itself. He writes that,

> in their artificiality and manifest constructedness, decadent collections foreground the logic of canon formation. Demonstrating how canons are made and what cultural and political

functions they perform, they challenge the assumption that the nation and its vernacular classics are joined in any natural or inevitable way. (214)

Just as the project of decadence destabilizes the classical canon, so too does the *giallo* genre foreground the instability of canonized cinematic modernism through the excessive articulation of its tropes. In taking up the mechanics of modernism and pushing them to the point of excess, the *giallo* genre signals the end of modernism—her last breath, and a moment of transition. Simultaneously, the decadent project resonates with the way the *giallo* disrupts the traditional canon of Italian national cinema through its transnational production and approach to language, its cosmopolitan global aesthetic, and the ways it draws on various formal influences to challenge taste cultures.

In the final shot of *Deep Red*, amateur detective Daly's face is reflected in the glass-like surface of a pool of blood. The blood's supremely lurid color points to the artifice of the scenario. The murderer is dead and the crime solved—there's nothing left to do, but the void that Daly has confronted refuses to dematerialize. The process of detection has propelled him, and us, to its conclusion, but there is no possibility of transcendence. As Kovács writes:

> The end of modernist art comes with the moment when the problem of nothingness disappears as a serious question, where nothingness is not discovered anymore behind the "scene," when nothingness is no longer a value, no longer the opposite dimension of being, no longer a power of transcendence, because common knowledge about "what is missing" no longer exists. (400)

If modernity is characterized by nostalgia for the past, the late modernity of the *giallo* feels more like dementia, one drenched with longing for a past it cannot quite remember.

Conclusion

FOUR YEARS AFTER THE RELEASE of their 2009 revisionist *giallo* film *Amer*, Hélène Cattet and Bruno Forzani returned to the genre in 2013 with *The Strange Color of Your Body's Tears*. Their second neo-*giallo* is about a man who returns from a business trip to discover his wife, Edwige, is missing. In the process of enquiring about her whereabouts, he becomes embroiled in a surreal nightmare that plays out in the apartments of his unknown neighbors and in the secret passages behind the walls of their building. Early in the film, compelled to uncover a way into this system of passageways, the man takes a hammer and smashes through the tiled wall of his bathroom. As the hammer comes into contact with the ceramic tiles, they shatter into sharp splinters and begin to reveal the mysterious cavernous spaces that lie behind the wall. The man breaks through to discover this passageway, but, for the *giallo* film fan, the sound these tiles make as they fall onto the bathroom floor opens up another passage—one that leads to the moment when David Hemmings's character Marcus Daly smashes through the plastered wall of the house with the singing child in Argento's *Deep Red*.

In fact, these wormholes back into Italian *giallo* films of the 1970s are opening up all the way through *The Strange Color of Your Body's Tears*, from the moment the film begins. Jason Anderson, in his review for *Cinema Scope*, suggests that its opening functions as "a primer on the semiotics of the *giallo* film," after which the directors "rapidly proceed down the lurid checklist of essential sights that no self-respecting exercise in the genre could do without." This checklist is the kind we've seen already: those fan-authored lists that include such motifs as black leather gloves, demented children's dolls, disembodied eyes, and the gleaming blade of a very sharp knife. Certainly, *The Strange Color of Your Body's Tears* has all of these, or what Anton Bitel refers to as "the grammar [and] iconography . . . of the sensationalist mystery genre known as *giallo*" (review of *Strange Colour*). Cattet and Forzani's film also directly quotes particular traditional *giallo* films: when their protagonist finds a pair of shiny red pumps in his missing wife's closet, *giallo* fans will understand the reference to Argento's *Tenebrae* immediately.

For Michael Atkinson, what Cattet and Forzani offer here is "a unique recipe for meta-giallo," but this is a recipe for formal style more than a list of motifs, one that involves "paintbox flourishes and slivered reflections, Art Nouveau designs, and stop-motion still montages, edited together in a rambunctious associative flow that doesn't tell a story so much as arterially spray one across a sumptuously papered wall." For Bitel, the directors' films work to "distil the language of *giallo* down to its sensory quintessence."

As the reviews of *The Strange Color of Your Body's Tears* illustrate, Cattet and Forzani's film draws on the meaning-making structures of the *giallo* to develop an index of a group of films that are clearly understood by these critics—and the filmmakers themselves—to constitute a genre. But the *giallo*, as it is conceived of in this 2013 film, is not the same set of structuring patterns as the one Italian *giallo* filmmakers and audiences in the 1970s understood. This traceable shift does not imply oppositional perspectives on a fixed body of texts, but is a symptom of how the indexicality of the *giallo* perpetually regenerates to open up a multiplicity of patterns of repetition and variation.

What both of Cattet and Forzani's neo-*giallo* films evidence is how subsequent audiences of the genre have facilitated the process of "regenrification" (Altman, *Film/Genre*). When these "formulaic" Italian films produced primarily in the 1970s begin to find a new audience a decade or so later with English-speaking horror video collectors, this body of texts is recontextualized by new reading strategies that diametrically oppose their earlier status as popular products designed for mass consumption. The *giallo*'s absorption into the canons of cult cinema in this period helps to concentrate and solidify the particular formation of the genre that a neo-*giallo* like *The Strange Color of Your Body's Tears* draws on. This formation of the *giallo* genre pivots on the work of directors like Mario Bava, Dario Argento, and Lucio Fulci. It solidifies around the recognizable patterns formed by the appearance and reappearance of the traumatized killer's black leather gloves, through a festishization of particular cinematic devices like voyeuristic pans and uncomfortable close-ups on eyes both human and animal. Because the genre's borders are messy and permeable, it absorbs tendencies from other generic trends these directors worked in, too. When, in *The Strange Color of Your Body's Tears*, Klaus Tange's character, Dan, looks through a car window into the night and sees a garishly illuminated city streetscape, the washes of heavily saturated red and green are reflections of Argento's 1977 supernatural horror film *Suspiria*. Similarly, the aesthetic of his highly ornate, motif-laden art nouveau apartment building and its labyrinthine skeleton of hidden corridors and passageways is lifted from *Suspiria*'s 1980 sequel *Inferno*—not one of Argento's contributions to the *giallo* genre. This cross-genre conflation works to fold Argento's use of nightmarish, saturated color in his horror films into the *giallo*'s emphasis on narratives of crime and detection, to generate an even more aggressively stylized image of the *giallo*—one that, in the case of *The Strange Color of Your Body's Tears* and its apartment building setting, literally explodes into kaleidoscopic reverie. Such reverie is nothing if not reflexive: in those moments when this film submits to the perpetually unfolding and transformative motion of the kaleidoscope's patterning by allowing it to overtake the photographic image, we experience simultaneously the genre's luminous, glassy aesthetic and a highly self-conscious image of genre's meaning-making processes.

The *giallo*, as it is conceived of here, is all of these as well as something in between. In other words, the *giallo* is understood here as a *critical category*. Like the classical Hollywood melodramas and crime films christened film noirs by French critics in the 1950s, the *giallo* here is understood as a category constituted retrospectively, functioning as a sign that points to a group of films with a roughly delineated, geographically specific, period of production. Once we unlock the *giallo* genre from the way (imagined) initial audiences read and used these films, a pattern of internal logic begins to surface across this body of texts—one that responds to the particular conditions of late modernity.

This working through of the tension and anxiety of modernity reflected in and interrogated by modernist art plays out most significantly in the *giallo*'s construction of the city and the experiences and ways of seeing it facilitates. Through their sustained examinations of the cinematic city and its architectural image, *giallo* films stress the senses of dispersion and disconnection that writers like Kracauer and Benjamin identify as the conditions of modernity. But unlike the literary detection narratives such writers argued were quintessentially modern, the late-modern *giallo* refuses to offer us the illusion of closure. The sense of loss that routinely dominates the *giallo* film's final moments is at odds with the discovery of the killer's identity and its implied restoration of order. Beneath the murder mystery narrative and the industrially conceived formula used to fashion these popular films, a ghostly sense of repetition and emptiness resonates. I have described this tone as being like the conditions of listening to a scratched vinyl record spinning on a turntable, where the stylus' forward momentum is continuously disrupted, revealing an inescapable schism. It is significant that Cattet and Forzani's neo-*giallo* uses this image of the perpetually spinning blackness of the record on the turntable, but Atkinson suggests that the neonoir *The Strange Color of Your Body's Tears* might be thought of as "a wry art installation/essay on modern anxieties, not an attempt at expressing them." The film revels in the decadent formal expression of this mode and its fetishization of surfaces, but what the wryness of this neo-*giallo* replaces is the traditional Italian *giallo*'s nostalgic near-forgotten desire for the restoration of order and a sense of communion. When the apartment next door to Cattet and Forzani's protagonist becomes the scene of a crime, we hear a shrill, anxious soundscape that foregrounds the horror of the bloody scene laid out on the living room floor. Suddenly, the police inspector yells for somebody to "switch the sound off—it's awful!" and a still-spinning turntable comes into shot. The turntable is switched off, and everything is quiet.

Works Cited

Altman, Rick. *Film/Genre*. British Film Institute, 1999.
———. "A Semantic/Syntactic Approach to Film Genre." *Cinema Journal*, vol. 23, no. 3, Spring 1984, pp. 6–18.
Ancy. Review of *The Pyjama Girl Case*, directed by Flavio Mogherini. *Variety*, 8 Feb. 1978, pp. 18, 34.
Anderson, Benedict. *Imagined Communities: Reflections on the Origin and Spread of Nationalism*. Rev. ed., Verso, 2006.
Anderson, Jason. "Black, White, and Giallo: Forzani and Cattet's *The Strange Colour of Your Body's Tears*." *Cinema Scope*, no. 63, Summer 2015, p. 45.
Andrews, Nigel. "A King-in-Waiting Gets His Plosives Fixed." *Financial Times*, 6 Jan. 2011.
Ascheid, Antje. "Speaking Tongues: Voice Dubbing in the Cinema as Cultural Ventriloquism." *Velvet Light Trap*, Fall 1997, pp. 32–41.
Atkinson, Michael. Review of *The Strange Colour of Your Body's Tears*, directed by Hélène Cattet and Bruno Forzani. *Film Comment*, vol. 50, no. 5, 2014, p. 70.
Baschiera, Stefano, and Francesco Di Chiara. "Once upon a Time in Italy: Transnational Features of Genre Production 1960s–1970s." *Film International*, vol. 8, no. 6, 2010, pp. 30–39.
Baudelaire, Charles. "The Seven Old Men." *The Flowers of Evil*. Oxford UP, 2008, pp. 177–80.
Bauman, Zygmunt. "From Pilgrim to Tourist—or a Short History of Identity." *Questions of Cultural Identity*, edited by Stuart Hall and Paul Du Gay, Sage, 1996, pp. 18–36.
Bazin, André. "An Aesthetic of Reality: Neorealism." *What Is Cinema?*, selected and translated by Hugh Gray, vol. 2, U of California P, 2004, pp. 16–40.
Bellour, Raymond. "On Fritz Lang." *SubStance*, vol. 3, no. 9, 1974, pp. 25–34. Translation, originally published in French as "Sur Fritz Lang," in *Critique*, no. 226, 1966.
Belton, John. "The Bionic Eye: Zoom Esthetics." *Cineaste*, vol. 11, no. 1, 1980, pp. 20–27.

Benjamin, Walter. *The Arcades Project*. Harvard UP, 2002.

———. *Illuminations*. Translated by Harry Zohn, Schocken, 1969.

———. "The Paris of the Second Empire in Baudelaire." *Selected Writings*, edited by Howard Eiland and Michael W. Jennings, vol. 4, Harvard UP, 2003, pp. 3–92.

Betz, Mark. "High and Low and In Between." *Screen*, vol. 54, no. 4, 2013, pp. 495–513.

Bitel, Anton. Review of *Amer*, directed by Hélène Cattet and Bruno Forzani. *Sight and Sound*, vol. 21, no. 2, 2011, pp. 46–47.

———. Review of *The Strange Colour of Your Body's Tears*, directed by Hélène Cattet and Bruno Forzani. *Sight and Sound*, vol. 24, no. 5, 2014, p. 66.

Bondanella, Peter E. *A History of the Italian Cinema*. New York: Continuum, 2009.

———. *Italian Cinema: From Neorealism to the Present*. 3rd ed., Continuum, 2001.

Bradbury, Malcom, and James McFarlane. "The Name and Nature of Modernism." *Modernism 1890–1930*, edited by Malcolm Bradbury and James McFarlane, Harvester Press / Humanities Press, 1978, pp. 19–55.

Brand, Dana. "From the *Flâneur* to the Detective: Interpreting the City of Poe." *Popular Fiction: Technology, Ideology, Production, Reading*, edited by Tony Bennett, Routledge, 1990, pp. 220–32.

Braudy, Leo. *Native Informant: Essays on Film, Fiction, and Popular Culture*. Oxford UP, 1991.

Brayton, Tim. "Summer of Blood: One Good Cop." *Antagony and Ecstasy*, 8 June 2009, http://reviews.antagonyecstasy.com/2009/06/summer-of-blood-one-good-cop.html?m=1.

Bruno, Giuliana. *Atlas of Emotion: Journeys in Art, Architecture, and Film*. Verso, 2002.

Burrell, Nigel J., and Paul J. Brown. *Giallo Scrapbook*. 2nd ed., Midnight Media, 2008.

Cain, James M. *The Postman Always Rings Twice*. Bloomsbury, 1997.

Canby, Vincent. "'Deep Red' Is a Bucket of Ax-Murder Cliches." *New York Times*, 10 June 1976.

Chippendale, Peter. "How High Street Horror Is Invading the Home." *Sunday Times*, 23 May 1982.

Church, David. "One on Top of the Other: Lucio Fulci, Transnational Film Industries, and the Retrospective Construction of the Italian Horror Canon." *Quarterly Review of Film and Video*, vol. 32, no. 1, 2015, pp. 1–20.

Combs, Richard. Review of *Cat O'Nine Tails*, directed by Dario Argento. *Monthly Film Bulletin*, July 1971, p. 120.

Crofts, Stephen. "Reconceptualizing National Cinema/s." *Film and Nationalism*, edited by Alan Williams, Rutgers UP, 2002, pp. 25–52.

Dickinson, Kay. "Troubling Synthesis: The Horrific Sights and Incompatible Sounds of the Video Nasties." *Sleaze Artists: Cinema at the Margins of Taste, Style, and Politics*, edited by Jeffrey Sconce, Duke UP, 2007, pp. 167–88.

"Dilettante." *The Oxford English Dictionary*. 2nd ed., 1989.

Dimendberg, Edward. "From Berlin to Bunker Hill: Urban Space, Late Modernity, and Film Noir in Fritz Lang's and Joseph Losey's M." *Wide Angle*, vol. 19, no. 4, 1997, pp. 62–93.

———. "The Will to Motorization: Cinema, Highways, and Modernity: For Wolf Donner, in Memoriam." *October*, vol. 73, Summer 1995, pp. 91–137.

Dunn, Jamie. Review of *Amer*, directed by Hélène Cattet and Bruno Forzani. *The Skinny*, 28 Dec. 2010, https://www.theskinny.co.uk/film/new-releases/amer-bitter.

Easthope, Anthony. "Cinecities of the Sixties." *The Cinematic City*, edited by David B. Clarke, Taylor and Francis, 1997, pp. 131–40.

Edmonstone, Robert J. *Beyond "Brutality": Understanding the Italian Filone's Violent Excesses*. 2008. U of Glasgow, PhD dissertation.

Egan, Kate. "The Celebration of a 'Proper Product': Exploring the Residual Collectible through the 'The Video Nasty.'" *Residual Media*, edited by Charles R. Acland, U of Minnesota P, 2007, pp. 200–21.

———. *Trash or Treasure? Censorship and the Changing Meanings of the Video Nasties*. Manchester UP, 2007.

Ehrenreich, Andreas. "Not Niche at All: The Distribution and Marketing of the 'Giallo' Genre." *Bianco e nero*, vol. 587, pp. 113–28.

Eleftheriotis, Dimitris. *Popular Cinemas of Europe: Studies of Texts, Contexts and Frameworks*, Continuum, 2001.

Eliot, T. S. "The Love Song of J. Alfred Prufrock." *Bartleby.com*, www.bartleby.com/198/1.html.

Elsaesser, Thomas. "Reflection and Reality: Narrative Cinema in the Concave Mirror." *Monogram*, no. 2, 1971, pp. 2–9.

Felski, Rita. *The Gender of Modernity*. Harvard UP, 1995.

Forster, E. M. *A Room with a View*. 1908. Penguin, 1990.

Frayling, Christopher. *Spaghetti Westerns: Cowboys and Europeans from Karl May to Sergio Leone*. Routledge, 1981.

Friedberg, Anne. *Window Shopping: Cinema and the Postmodern*. U of California P, 1993.

Friedman, Susan Stanford. "Definitional Excursions: The Meanings of Modern/Modernity/Modernism." *Modernism/modernity*, vol. 8, no. 3, 2001, pp. 493–513.

Frisby, David. "Between the Spheres: Siegfried Kracauer and the Detective Novel." *Theory, Culture and Society*, vol. 9, no. 2, 1992, pp. 1–22.

———. *Fragments of Modernity: Theories of Modernity in the Work of Simmel, Kracauer and Benjamin*. Polity, 1986.

Fujiwara, Chris. "Boredom, *Spasmo* and the Italian System." *Sleaze Artists: Cinema at the Margins of Taste, Style and Politics*, edited by Jeffrey Sconce, Duke UP, 240–58.

Fuoco, Robert. "'They Affect Dogs as Well'—Crime and British Video Censorship in the Early 1980s." *Offscreen*, vol. 20, no. 12, 2016, https://offscreen.com/view/british-video-censorship-1980s.

Goldmark, Daniel, Lawrence Kramer, and Richard Leppert, editors. *Beyond the Soundtrack: Representing Music in Cinema*. U of California P, 2007.
Gracey, James. *Dario Argento*. Kamera, 2010.
Gray, Noel. "The Kaleidoscope: Shake, Rattle and Roll." *Continuum*, vol. 6, no. 2, 1993, pp. 95–106.
Guins, Raiford. "Blood and Black Gloves on Shiny Discs: New Media, Old Tastes, and the Remediation of Italian Horror Films in the United States." *Horror International*, edited by Steven Jay Schneider and Tony Williams, Wayne State UP, 2005, pp. 15–32. Contemporary Approaches to Film and Television.
Gunning, Tom. "From the Kaleidoscope to the X-Ray: Urban Spectatorship, Poe, Benjamin, and *Traffic in Souls* (1913)." *Wide Angle*, vol. 19, no. 4, 1997, pp. 25–61.
Haaland, Torunn. "Strolling the Streets of Modernity: Experiences of Flanerie and Cityscapes in Italian Postward Film." 2007. Indiana U, PhD dissertation.
Hawkins, Joan. *Cutting Edge: Art-Horror and the Horrific Avant-Garde*. U of Minnesota P, 2000.
Hayward, Susan. "Framing National Cinema." *Cinema and Nation*, edited by Mette Hjort and Scott MacKenzie, Routledge, 2000, pp. 88–102.
Herzog, Todd. *Crime stories: Criminalistic Fantasy and the Culture of Crisis in Weimar Germany*. Berghahn Books, 2009. Monographs in German History 22.
Higson, Andrew. "The Limiting Imagination of the National Cinema." *Cinema and Nation*, edited by Mette Hjort and Scott MacKenzie, Routledge, 2000, pp. 63–74.
———. *Waving the Flag: Constructing a National Cinema in Britain*. Oxford UP, 1995.
Hitchcock, Henry-Russell, and Philip Johnson. *The International Style*. New ed., W. W. Norton, 1996.
Holden, Stephen. "Ogled and Threatened on a Journey to Womanhood." *New York Times*, 29 October 2010.
Hunt, Leon. "A (Sadistic) Night at the Opera: Notes on the Italian Horror Film." *Velvet Light Trap*, Fall 1992, pp. 65–76.
Hunter, Russ. "'Didn't You Used to Be Dario Argento?' The Cult Reception of Dario Argento." *Italian Film Directors in the New Millennium*, edited by William Hope, Cambridge Scholars Press, 2010, pp. 63–74.
Jancovich, Mark. "Cult Fictions: Cult Movies, Subcultural Capital and the Production of Cultural Distinctions." *Cultural Studies*, vol. 16, no. 2, 2002, pp. 306–22.
Johnson, Paul. "Terrore Italiani: Classical Detective Fiction and the Giallo." *Saturn in Retrograde*, 2011, http://cultreels.blogspot.com.au/search?q=giallo.
Kannas, Alexia. *Deep Red*. Columbia UP, 2017.
Klinger, Barbara. *Beyond the Multiplex: Cinema, New Technologies, and the Home*. U of California P, 2006.
———. "'Cinema/Ideology/Criticism' Revisited: The Progressive Genre." *Film Genre Reader*, edited by Barry Keith Grant, U of Texas P, 1986, pp. 74–90.

———. "The New Media Aristocrats: Home Theater and the Domestic Film Experience." *Velvet Light Trap*, Fall 1998, pp. 4–20.
Koch, Gertrud. *Siegfried Kracauer: An Introduction*. Translated by Jeremy Gaines, Princeton UP, 2000.
Kovacs, András Bálint. *Screening Modernism: European Art Cinema, 1950–1980*. U of Chicago P, 2007.
Koven, Mikel J. *La Dolce Morte: Vernacular Cinema and the Italian Giallo Film*. Scarecrow Press, 2006.
Kracauer, Siegfried. "The Hotel Lobby." *Rethinking Architecture: A Reader in Cultural Theory*, edited by Neil Leach, Routledge, 1997, pp. 50–62.
———. "Those Who Wait." *The Mass Ornament: Weimar Essays*, edited by Thomas Y. Levin, Harvard UP, 1995, pp. 129–40.
Landy, Marcia. *Italian Film*. Cambridge UP, 2000. National Film Traditions.
Lanza, Joseph. "My Aisles of Golden Dreams: The Beauty of Supermarket Music." *Cinesonic: Cinema and the Sound of Music*, edited by Philip Brophy, Australian Film Television and Radio School / Allen and Unwin, 2000, pp. 59–80.
Le Corbusier. *Toward an Architecture*. Getty Research Institute, 2007.
Levy, Mark R., editor. *The VCR Age: Home Video and Mass Communication*. Sage, 1989.
Leyland, Matthew. Review of *The House with Laughing Windows*, directed by Pupi Avati. *Sight and Sound*, vol. 16, no. 11, 2006, p. 89.
Luhr, William, and Peter Lehman. "*Experiment in Terror*: Dystopian Modernism, the Police Procedural, and the Space of Anxiety." *Cinema and Modernity*, edited by Murray Pomerance, Rutgers UP, 2006, pp. 175–93.
Marcus, Millicent. *After Fellini: National Cinema in the Postmodern Age*. Johns Hopkins UP, 2002.
Martin, Adrian, and Jonathan Rosenbaum, editors. *Movie Mutations: The Changing Face of World Cinephilia*. British Film Institute, 2003.
McGillivray, David. Review of *Evil Fingers* [also *Fifth Cord*]. *Monthly Film Bulletin*, November 1973, p. 227.
Met, Philippe. "'Knowing Too Much' about Hitchcock: The Genesis of the Italian Giallo." *After Hitchcock: Influence, Imitation and Intertextuality*, edited by David Boyd and R. Barton Palmer, U of Texas P, 2006, pp. 195–214.
Moine, Raphaëlle. *Cinema Genre*. Blackwell, 2008.
Moretti, Franco. "Clues." *Popular Fiction: Technology, Ideology, Production, Reading*, edited by Tony Bennett, Routledge, 1990, pp. 220–37.
Morley, Neville. "Decadence as a Theory of History." *New Literary History*, vol. 35, no. 4, 2004, pp. 573–85.
Neale, Steve. "Westerns and Gangster Films since the 1970s." *Genre and Contemporary Hollywood*, edited by Steve Neal, British Film Institute, 2002, pp. 27–47.
Needham, Gary. "Playing with Genre: An Introduction to the Italian *Giallo*." *Kinoeye*, vol. 2, no. 11, 2002, http://www.kinoeye.org/02/11/needham11.php.

———. "Playing with Genre: Defining the Italian *Giallo*." *Fear without Frontiers: Horror Cinema across the Globe*, edited by Steven Jay Schneider, FAB, 2003, pp. 135–44.

Newman, Kim. "Journal of the Plague Years." *Screen Violence*, edited by Karl French, Bloomsbury, 1996, pp. 132–43.

Olesen, Giulio. "An Interview with Sergio Martino: An American in Rome." *Journal of Italian Cinema and Media Studies*, vol. 5, no. 2, 2017, pp. 261–66.

Perry, Ted, editor. *Masterpieces of Modernist Cinema*. Indiana UP, 2006.

Pirie, David. Review of *The Black Belly of the Tarantula*, directed by Paolo Cavara. *Monthly Film Bulletin*, March 1973, p. 56.

Poe, Edgar Allan. "The Man of the Crowd." *Complete Stories and Poems of Edgar Allan Poe*, Doubleday, 1966, pp. 215–21.

Potolsky, Matthew. "Decadence, Nationalism, and the Logic of Canon Formation." *Modern Language Quarterly*, vol. 67, no. 2, 2006, pp. 213–44.

Rodrigues, Chris, and Chris Garrett. *Introducing Modernism*. Icon, 2004.

Salzani, Carlo. *Constellations of Reading: Walter Benjamin in Figures of Actuality*. Peter Lang, 2009.

Sanjek, David. "Fans' Notes: The Horror Film Fanzine." *Literature/Film Quarterly*, vol. 18, no. 3, 1990, pp. 150–59.

Schatz, Thomas. *Hollywood Genres: Formulas, Filmmaking, and the Studio System*. Temple UP, 1981.

Sconce, Jeffrey. "'Trashing' the Academy: Taste, Excess, and an Emerging Politics of Cinematic Style." *Screen*, vol. 36, no. 4, 1995, pp. 371–93.

Sexton, Jamie. "Creeping Decay: Cult Soundtracks, Residual Media, and Digital Technologies." *New Review of Film and Television Studies*, vol. 13, no. 1, 2015, pp. 12–30.

Shaya, Gregory. "The Flaneur, the Badaud, and the Making of a Mass Public in France, circa 1860–1910." *American Historical Review*, vol. 109, no. 1, 2004, pp. 41–77.

Shochat, Ella, and Robert Stam. "The Cinema after Babel: Language, Difference, Power." *Screen*, vol. 26, no. 3–4, 1985, pp. 35–58.

Staiger, Janet. "Hybrid or Inbred: The Purity Hypothesis and Hollywood Genre History." *Film Criticism*, vol. 22, no. 1, 1997, 5–20.

Stam, Robert. *Reflexivity in Film and Literature*. UMI Research Press, 1985.

Thain, Marion. "Modernist 'Homage' to the 'Fin De Siècle.'" *Yearbook of English Studies*, vol. 37, no. 1, 2007, pp. 22–40.

Tooze, Gary W. Review of *The Bird with the Crystal Plumage*, Arrow Video 2017 Blu-ray release, http://www.dvdbeaver.com/film2/DVDReviews44/bird_with_the_crystal_plumage_blu-ray.htm.

———. Review of *Blood and Black Lace*, DVD and Blu-ray releases, http://www.dvdbeaver.com/film5/blu-ray_reviews_67/blood_and_black_lace_blu-ray.htm.

———. Review of *The Fifth Cord*, Arrow Video 2019 Blu-ray release, http://www.dvdbeaver.com/film6/dvd_reviews_67/the_fifth_cord_blu-ray.htm.

Urry, John. *The Tourist Gaze*. 2nd ed., Sage, 2002.

Vidler, Anthony. *Warped Space: Art, Architecture, and Anxiety in Modern Culture.* MIT P, 2000.
Wagstaff, Christopher. "A Forkful of Westerns: Industry, Audiences and the Italian Western." *Popular European Cinema*, edited by Richard Dyer and Ginette Vincendeau, Routledge, 1992, pp. 245–61.
Weir, David. *Decadence and the Making of Modernism.* U of Massachusetts P, 1996.
Willemen, Paul. "The Zoom in Popular Cinema: A Question of Performance." *Inter-Asia Cultural Studies*, vol. 14, no. 1, 2013, pp. 104–09.
Williams, Alan. "Is a Radical Genre Criticism Possible?" *Quarterly Review of Film Studies*, vol. 9, no. 2, 1984, pp. 121–25.
Williams, Linda Ruth. "An Eye for an Eye." *Sight and Sound*, vol. 4, no. 4, 1994, pp. 14–16.
Wood, Jason. *Last Words: Considering Contemporary Cinema.* Columbia UP, 2014.
Wood, Mary P. *Italian Cinema.* Eng. ed., Berg, 2005.
———. "Italian Film Noir." *European Film Noir*, edited by Andrew Spicer, Manchester UP, 2007, pp. 23–72.
Wood, Robin. "Ideology, Genre, Auteur." *Film Genre Reader II*, edited by Barry Keith Grant, U of Texas P, 1995, pp. 59–73.
Worland, Rick. *The Horror Film: An Introduction.* Blackwell, 2007. New Approaches to Film Genre.

Filmography

Alphaville. Jean-Luc Godard, 1964.
All the Colors of the Dark [*Tutti i colori del buio*; also *They're Coming to Get You* (USA); *Day of the Maniac* (USA); *Demons of the Dead* (USA)]. Sergio Martino, 1972.
Amer. Hélène Cattet and Bruno Forzani, 2009.
Anguish. Bigas Luna, 1980.
Back to the Future III. Robert Zemeckis, 1990.
Badlands. Terrence Malick, 1973.
A Bay of Blood [*Ecologia del delitto*; also *Twitch of the Death Nerve* (USA)]. Mario Bava, 1971.
Berberian Sound Studio. Peter Strickland, 2012.
The Beyond [. . . *E tu vivrai nel terrore! L'aldilà*; also *7 Doors of Death* (USA)]. Lucio Fulci, 1981.
The Bird with the Crystal Plumage [*L'uccello dalle piume di cristallo*; also *The Gallery Murders* (UK)]. Dario Argento, 1970.
Black Belly of the Tarantula [*La tarantola dal ventre nero*]. Paolo Cavara, 1971.
A Black Veil for Lisa [*La morte non ha sesso*]. Massimo Dallamano, 1968.
A Blade in the Dark [*La casa con la scala nel buio*; also *The House with the Dark Staircase* (literal)]. Lamberto Bava, 1983.
Blood and Black Lace [*Sei donne per l'assassino*; also *Six Women for the Murderer* (literal)]. Mario Bava, 1964.
The Bloodstained Shadow [*Solamente nero*; also *Only Blackness* (literal)]. Antonio Bido, 1978.
Blow-Up. Michelangelo Antonioni, 1966.
The Burning. Tony Maylam, 1981.
The Case Of The Bloody Iris [*Perché quelle strane gocce di sangue sul corpo di Jennifer?*; also *What Are Those Strange Drops of Blood Doing on Jennifer's Body?* (literal)]. Giuliano Carnimeo, 1972.
The Case of the Scorpion's Tail [*La coda dello scorpione*]. Sergio Martino, 1971.
The Conformist [*Il conformista*]. Bernardo Bertolucci, 1970.
Curse of the Undead. Edward Dein, 1959.

Death Laid an Egg [*La morte ha fatto l'uovo*; also *A Curious Way to Love* (Ireland)]. Guilio Questi, 1968.
Death Walks on High Heels [*La morte cammina con i tacchi alti*]. Luciano Ercoli, 1971.
Deep Red [*Profondo rosso*; also *The Hatchet Murders* (USA)]. Dario Argento, 1975.
Dellamorte Dellamore [also *Cemetery Man* (USA); *Of Death and Love* (Australia)]. Michele Soavi, 1994.
Don't Torture a Duckling [*Non si sevizia un paperino*; also *Don't Torture Donald Duck* (literal)]. Lucio Fulci, 1972.
Door into Darkness [*La porta sul buio*]. Dario Argento, Luigi Cozzi, Mario Foglietti, Roberto Pariante, 1973. TV.
Do You Like Hitchcock? [*Ti piace Hitchcock?*]. Dario Argento, 2005.
Dr. No. Terence Young, 1962.
The Fifth Cord [*Giornata nera per l'ariete*; also *Evil Fingers* (USA)]. Luigi Bazzoni, 1971.
Five Dolls for an August Moon [*5 bambole per la luna d'agosto*; also *Island of Terror* (USA alternative title)]. Mario Bava, 1970.
Four Flies on Grey Velvet [*4 mosche di velluto grigio*]. Dario Argento, 1971.
The Girl Who Knew Too Much [*La ragazza che sapeva troppo*; also *The Evil Eye* (USA)]. Mario Bava, 1962.
The Graduate. Mike Nichols, 1967.
Hostel. Eli Roth, 2005.
The House of the Laughing Windows [*La casa dalle finestre che ridono*]. Pupi Avati, 1976.
Inferno. Dario Argento, 1980.
L'Avventura. Michelangelo Antonioni, 1960.
La Dolce Vita. Federico Fellini, 1960.
Opera [also *Terror at the Opera* (USA)]. Dario Argento, 1987.
Ossessione [also *Obsession* (literal)]. Luchino Visconti, 1943.
The Perfume of the Lady in Black [*Il profumo della signora in nero*]. Francesco Barilli, 1974.
Phenomena [also *Creepers* (USA)]. Dario Argento, 1985.
The Pyjama Girl Case [*La ragazza dal pigiama giallo*]. Flavio Mogherini, 1977.
Rome, Open City [*Roma citta aperta*]. Roberto Rossellini, 1945.
Short Night of the Glass Dolls [*La corta note delle bambole di vetro*; also *Paralyzed* (USA)]. Aldo Lado, 1971.
Sleepless. Dario Argento, 2001.
Spasmo. Umberto Lenzi, 1974.
Stealing Beauty. Bernardo Bertolucci, 1996.
The Strange Color of Your Body's Tears [*L'étrange couleur des larmes de ton corps*]. Hélène Cattet and Bruno Forzani, 2013.
The Strange Vice of Mrs. Wa`rdh [*Lo strano vizio della signora Wardh*]. Sergio Martino, 1971.
Suspiria. Dario Argento, 1977.
Tenebrae. Dario Argento, 1982.

Terror in the Crypt [*La cripta e l'incubo*; also *Crypt of the Vampire* (USA)]. Camillo Mastrocinque, 1964.
The Terror of Tiny Town. Sam Newfield, 1938.
Torso [*I corpi presentano tracce di violenza carnale*; also *The Bodies Show Traces of Carnal Violence* (literal)]. Sergio Martino, 1973.
Umberto D. Vitorio De Sica, 1952.
Un Chien Andalou [also *An Andalusian Dog* (literal)]. Luis Buñuel, 1929.
Vertigo. Alfred Hitchcock, 1958.
The Wizard of Gore. Herschell Gordon Lewis, 1970.
The Wizard of Oz. Victor Fleming, 1939.
What Have They Done to Your Daughters? [*La polizia chiede aiuto*]. Massimo Dallamano, 1974.
What Have You Done to Solange? [*Cosa avete fatto a Solange?*; also *Terror in the Woods* (USA)]. Massimo Dallamano, 1972.
Who Saw Her Die? [*Chi l'ha vista morire?*]. Aldo Lado, 1972.
Your Vice Is a Locked Room and Only I Have the Key [*Il tuo vizio è una stanza chiusa e solo io ne ho la chiave*]. Sergio Martino, 1972.

Index

Against Nature, 144
Alabiso, Eugenio, 59
Alphaville (Jean-Luc Godard, 1964), 99
Altman, Rick, 6, 7, 11, 13, 30–31, 34–35, 40, 43, 48, 148
Amer (Hélène Cattet and Bruno Forzani, 2009), 1–2, 4, 147
Anderson, Benedict, 18–19, 42
Anguish (Bigas Luna, 1987), 132
Antonioni, Michelangelo, 5, 11, 14, 78, 115
Argento, Dario, 4–7, 14, 21–22, 25, 27–28, 31, 33–34, 39, 42–63, 79, 82–85, 91, 97–99, 103–15, 119–121, 130–131, 135–139, 144, 147–149
Arrow Video, 58–59
Ascheid, Antje, 136
Avati, Pupi, 121

badaud, 103–108, 113, 116
Badlands (Terrence Malick, 1973), 87
Barilli, Francesco, 22, 23
Baschiera, Stefano, 21, 137
Bava, Lamberto, 144
Bava, Mario, 3–4, 6, 9–11, 13–14, 23, 28, 29, 31, 33, 45, 57, 90–91, 94, 106, 107, 116, 121, 134, 135, 140–141, 148

Bay of Blood, A (Mario Bava, 1971), 45
Baudelaire, Charles, 100, 105, 143
Bauman, Zygmunt, 96
Bazzoni, Luigi, 7, 59, 67
Bellour, Raymond, 129
Belton, John, 133, 135
Benjamin, Walter, 54, 76, 83–84, 92, 98, 100–102, 104, 108, 110–113, 149
Bertolucci, Bernardo, 89
Betz, Mark, 22
Beyond, The (Lucio Fulci, 1981), 5, 45
Bido, Antonio, 28
Bird with the Crystal Plumage, The (Dario Argento, 1970), 4, 7, 21, 33, 41, 55, 58–59, 91, 97, 99, 103–104, 112–116
Black Belly of the Tarantula (Paolo Cavara, 1971), 7, 23, 25, 67, 71–73, 77–79, 86–87, 121, 127
Blade in the Dark, A (Lamberto Bava, 1983), 144
Blood and Black Lace (Mario Bava, 1964), 9–10, 33, 57, 121
Bloodstained Shadow, The (Antonio Bido, 1978), 28
Blow Up (Michelangelo Antonioni, 1966), 78, 99
Bond, James, 99
Bondanella, Peter, 14–16, 22, 24, 27

Bradbury, Malcolm, 124
Brand, Dana, 109–110
Braudy, Leo, 131
Brecht, Bertolt, 110–111
Bruno, Guiliana, 7
Buñuel, Luis, 49
Burning, The (Tony Maylam, 1981), 4

Cain, James M., 16
Calandra, Guiliana, 131
Cannibal Holocaust (Ruggero Deodato, 1980), 45, 142
Carnimeo, Giuliano, 7, 28, 31, 65, 67, 134
Case Of The Bloody Iris, The (Giuliano Carnimeo, 1972), 7, 28, 31, 65–67, 70, 71, 77
Case of the Scorpion's Tail, The (Sergio Martino, 1971), 61–62
Castallari, Enzo, 42
Cattet, Hélène, 1, 27–28, 147–150
Cavara, Paolo, 7, 23, 67, 1270
Celentano, Adriano, 91
Christie, Agatha, 2
Church, David, 21, 29, 41, 58
cinephilia, 62
Criterion Collection, 59
Crofts, Stephen, 18, 20
Curse of the Undead (Edward Dein, 1959), 33

De Sica, Vittorio, 16, 17
Des Esseintes, 144
Death Laid an Egg (Guilio Questi, 1968), 55, 132
Death Waltz Records, 61–62
Deep Red (Dario Argento, 1975), 4, 9, 27, 40, 46–47, 58, 60, 115, 121, 130–131, 135–139, 145
Dein, Edward, 33
Dellamorte, Dellamore (Michele Soavi, 1994), 4
Di Chiara, Francesco, 21, 137
Dickinson, Kay, 135, 139, 142

Dimendberg, Edward, 7, 69–71, 75–77, 79
Dr. No (Terence Young, 1962), 99

Egan, Kate, 45–47, 53–54, 135
Ehrenreich, Andreas, 42–43
Edmonstone, Robert, 17, 22
Eleftheriotis, Dimitris, 11, 24–25, 36
Eliot, T. S., 109
Elsaesser, Thomas, 127
Ercoli, Luciano, 42
excess, 79, 120–123, 130, 143, 145
European art cinema, 4, 5, 8, 11, 22, 34, 115, 122, 127

fanzines, 44, 48–51, 55, 62, 63
Fascism, 3, 16, 17
Fellini, Federico, 5, 11, 14, 17, 98
Felski, Rita, 124
Fenech, Edwige, 134, 135
Fifth Cord, The (Luigi Bazzoni, 1971), 59, 67, 67–68, 70, 73–75, 82–86
film noir, 69–70, 75–77, 128–130
Five Dolls for an August Moon (Mario Bava, 1970), 135, 140–141
flâneur, 8, 92, 100–105, 108–110
Forster, E. M., 89, 96
Forzani, Bruno, 1, 27–28, 147–150
Four Flies on Grey Velvet (Dario Argento, 1971), 22, 55–56
Franco, Jesus, 133
Frayling, Christopher, 15
Friedman, Susan Standford, 8, 122, 127, 142
Frisby, David, 82–84, 98, 116
Fulci, Lucio, 6, 42, 45, 63, 148
Fuoco, Robert, 44

Garrette, Chris, 123–124
Gautier, Theophile, 143
genre: and
  evolutionary approach, 31–34
  Hollywood cinema, 11–15, 20–24, 30

hybridity, 12, 20, 23–25, 35
semantic/syntactic approach, 22, 29–31, 34
giallo (literary), 2, 3, 29, 34, 62
Giannini, Giancarlo, 23, 71, 86
Girl Who Knew Too Much, The (Mario Bava, 1962), 29, 33, 73, 90–96, 106–117
Goblin (band), 60, 80, 135, 139
Godard, Jean-Luc, 99
gothic, 10, 63, 143
Gracey, James, 25, 121
Graduate, The (Mike Nichols, 1967), 99
Guadagnino, Luca, 39
Guins, Raiford, 40, 54, 59, 62
Gunning, Tom, 9, 102–105, 115

Haaland, Torunn, 93, 100–102
Hayward, Susan, 14, 34
Heller-Nicholas, Alexandra, 59
Hemmings, David, 78, 115, 147
Herzog, Todd, 110–111, 113
Higson, Andrew, 18–20, 25, 34
Hitchcock, Alfred, 3, 29, 132
Hitchcock, Henry-Russell, 74–75
Holmes, Sherlock, 2, 101, 110
Hostel (Eli Roth, 2005), 119
House of the Laughing Windows, The (Pupi Avati, 1976), 121
Hunt, Leon, 52
Hunter, Russ, 39, 43
Huysmans, Joris-Karl, 143

Inferno (Dario Argento, 1980), 45, 149
imagined community, 18–19, 34, 42
International Style (architecture), 74–75, 82

Jameson, Frederic, 68
Jancovich, Mark, 52–53, 55
Johnson, Paul, 112, 113, 114
Johnson, Philip, 74

Kael, Pauline, 52
kaleidoscope, 9–13, 24–25, 35–37, 149
Klinger, Barbera, 58–60, 71
Koch, Gertrud, 112
Kovács, András Bálint 124–125, 145
Koven, Mikel, 21–34, 40–42, 53, 75, 87, 92, 97–100, 121, 128, 134, 144
Kracauer, Siegfried, 7, 66–67, 76, 85, 92, 110–113, 116, 149
krimi, 29

Lado, Aldo, 23, 28, 70, 98, 132
Landy, Marcia, 16
Lanza, Joseph, 140
L'Avventura (Michelangelo Antonioni, 1960), 99
La Dolce Vita (Federico Fellini, 1960), 98
Le Corbusier, 74–75
Lehman, Peter, 128–130
Lenzi, Umberto, 45, 134, 137
Leone, Sergio, 15
Levy, Mark, 44
Lewis, Herschell Gordon, 51
Lovesong of J. Alfred Prufrock, 109
Luhr, William, 128–130

Malick, Terrence, 87
Martin, Adrian, 62
Martino, Sergio, 39, 42, 61
Marsillach, Christina, 119
Marx, Karl, 83
Maylam, Tony, 4
McFarlane, James, 124
Méril, Macha, 132
Met, Philippe, 35
Modernism, 68, 70–71, 122–145
Mogherini, Flavio, 133
Moine, Raphaelle, 26, 32
Mondadori, 28, 62
Monti, Silvia, 82
Morely, Neville, 143–144
Moretti, Franco, 101, 109–113

Morricone, Ennio, 23, 60, 71–73, 135
Musak, 140
Mussolini, Benito 3, 17

Needham, Gary, 28, 98, 113–114
Neorealism, 11, 16–19
Nero, Franco, 67–68
Newfield, Sam, 33
Newman, Kim, 46–47
Nichols, Mike, 99
Nicolai, Bruno, 60, 61, 65, 135
Nicolodi, Daria, 131

Olesen, Giulio, 42
Opera (Dario Argento, 1987), 47, 119–120, 131
Ortolani, Riz, 60
Ossessione (Luchino Visconti, 1943), 16

Paracinema, 48–53
peplum, 22
Perfume of the Lady in Black, The (Francesco Barilli, 1974), 22–23, 30
Perry, Ted, 122, 125–129, 132, 139, 142
Petri, Elio, 18
Poe, Edgar Allan, 2, 97, 102–104, 106, 109–110, 143
Polanski, Roman, 22
Poliziotto (Italian police procedural), 15, 22, 23
Potolsky, Matthew, 144
Profondo Rosso (comic book), 51
Pyjama Girl Case, The (Flavio Mogherini, 1977), 133

Questi, Guilio, 55, 132

Ricoeur, Paul, 35–36
Rodrigues, Chris, 123–124
Roman, Leticia, 90
Rome, Open City (Roberto Rossellini, 1945), 17

Room with a View, A (novel), 89
Rossellini, Roberto, 17

Salzani, Carlo, 96–97
Sandrelli, Stefania, 86
Sanjek, David, 48
Saxon, John, 91
SBS (Special Broadcasting Service), 4
Schatz, Thomas, 11–12, 26, 32–33, 41
Sconce, Jeffrey, 48–53, 62
Shaya, Gregory, 105, 108–9
Sheen, Martin, 87
Shochat, Ella, 136
Short Night of the Glass Dolls (Aldo Lado, 1971), 28, 132
Simmel, Georg, 98
Sirk, Douglas, 116
slasher films, 4, 45, 48, 121
Sleepless (Dario Argento, 2001), 98, 144
Soavi, Michele, 4
soundtrack: and function 135–142
    vinyl releases 60–62
Spacek, Sissy, 87
spaghetti western, 15, 20, 21, 24
Spasmo (Umberto Lenzi, 1974), 134, 137
Staiger, Janet, 24, 35, 36, 37
Stam, Robert, 136, 138
Stealing Beauty (Bernardo Bertolucci, 1996), 89
Strange Color of Your Body's Tears, The (Hélène Cattet and Bruno Forzani, 2013), 27–28, 147–150
Strickland, Peter, 60
Suspiria (Dario Argento, 1977), 39, 46, 60, 149
Suspiria (Luca Guadagnino, 2019), 39

Tange, Klaus, 149
Tenebrae (Dario Argento, 1982), 28, 45, 67, 70, 79–82, 84–86, 114, 135, 142, 148
Thain, Marion, 143

The Terror of Tiny Town (Sam
    Newfield, 1938), 33
Thompson, Kristin, 120–122
tourist gaze, 92–95
Tyler, Liv, 89

Umberto D (Vitorio De Sica, 1952), 16
Un Chien Andalou (Luis Buñuel,
    1929), 119
Urry, John, 92–95

Vertigo (Alfred Hitchcock, 1958), 132
video nasties, 44–48, 53, 135
Vidler, Anthony, 66–67
Visconti, Luchino, 11, 16, 17

Wagstaff, Christopher, 17, 21, 26,
    40–43

Wallace, Edgar, 2
Weir, David, 143–144
Wendel, Lara, 84
West, Jake, 46
Willemen, Paul, 133
Williams, Linda Ruth, 119
Wizard of Oz, The (Victor Fleming,
    1939), 86
Who Saw Her Die? (Aldo Lado,
    1972), 23, 28, 70, 98
Wood, Ed, 49
Wood, Mary, 28, 70, 74, 76
Wood, Robin, 37

yellow-backs, 2
Young, Terence, 99

Zoom shot, 6, 133–135

Also in the series

William Rothman, editor, *Cavell on Film*

J. David Slocum, editor, *Rebel Without a Cause*

Joe McElhaney, *The Death of Classical Cinema*

Kirsten Moana Thompson, *Apocalyptic Dread*

Frances Gateward, editor, *Seoul Searching*

Michael Atkinson, editor, *Exile Cinema*

Paul S. Moore, *Now Playing*

Robin L. Murray and Joseph K. Heumann, *Ecology and Popular Film*

William Rothman, editor, *Three Documentary Filmmakers*

Sean Griffin, editor, *Hetero*

Jean-Michel Frodon, editor, *Cinema and the Shoah*

Carolyn Jess-Cooke and Constantine Verevis, editors, *Second Takes*

Matthew Solomon, editor, *Fantastic Voyages of the Cinematic Imagination*

R. Barton Palmer and David Boyd, editors, *Hitchcock at the Source*

William Rothman, *Hitchcock: The Murderous Gaze, Second Edition*

Joanna Hearne, *Native Recognition*

Marc Raymond, *Hollywood's New Yorker*

Steven Rybin and Will Scheibel, editors, *Lonely Places, Dangerous Ground*

Claire Perkins and Constantine Verevis, editors, *B Is for Bad Cinema*

Dominic Lennard, *Bad Seeds and Holy Terrors*

Rosie Thomas, *Bombay before Bollywood*

Scott M. MacDonald, *Binghamton Babylon*

Sudhir Mahadevan, *A Very Old Machine*

David Greven, *Ghost Faces*

James S. Williams, *Encounters with Godard*

William H. Epstein and R. Barton Palmer, editors, *Invented Lives, Imagined Communities*

Lee Carruthers, *Doing Time*

Rebecca Meyers, William Rothman, and Charles Warren, editors, *Looking with Robert Gardner*

Belinda Smaill, *Regarding Life*

Douglas McFarland and Wesley King, editors, *John Huston as Adaptor*

R. Barton Palmer, Homer B. Pettey, and Steven M. Sanders, editors, *Hitchcock's Moral Gaze*

Nenad Jovanovic, *Brechtian Cinemas*

Will Scheibel, *American Stranger*

Amy Rust, *Passionate Detachments*

Steven Rybin, *Gestures of Love*

Seth Friedman, *Are You Watching Closely?*

Roger Rawlings, *Ripping England!*

Michael DeAngelis, *Rx Hollywood*

Ricardo E. Zulueta, *Queer Art Camp Superstar*

John Caruana and Mark Cauchi, editors, *Immanent Frames*

Nathan Holmes, *Welcome to Fear City*

Homer B. Pettey and R. Barton Palmer, editors, *Rule, Britannia!*

Milo Sweedler, *Rumble and Crash*

Ken Windrum, *From El Dorado to Lost Horizons*

Matthew Lau, *Sounds Like Helicopters*

Dominic Lennard, *Brute Force*

William Rothman, *Tuitions and Intuitions*

Michael Hammond, *The Great War in Hollywood Memory, 1918–1939*

Burke Hilsabeck, *The Slapstick Camera*

Niels Niessen, *Miraculous Realism*

Alex Clayton, *Funny How?*

Bill Krohn, *Letters from Hollywood*

www.ingramcontent.com/pod-product-compliance
Lightning Source LLC
Chambersburg PA
CBHW021143230426
43667CB00005B/229